T&T CLARK STUDY GUIDES TO THE NEW TESTAMENT

1 & 2 Thessalonians

Series Editor
Tat-siong Benny Liew, College of the Holy Cross, USA

T0347713

1 & 2 THESSALONIANS

An Introduction and Study Guide
Encountering the Christ Group at Thessalonike

By
Richard S. Ascough

Bloomsbury T&T Clark
An imprint of Bloomsbury Publishing Plc

B L O O M S B U R Y
LONDON • OXFORD • NEW YORK • NEW DELHI • SYDNEY

Bloomsbury T&T Clark
An imprint of Bloomsbury Publishing Plc

Imprint previously known as T&T Clark

50 Bedford Square	1385 Broadway
London	New York
WC1B 3DP	NY 10018
UK	USA

www.bloomsbury.com

**BLOOMSBURY, T&T CLARK and the Diana logo are trademarks of
Bloomsbury Publishing Plc**

First published 2014. This edition published 2017

British Library Cataloguing-in-Publication Data
A catalogue record for this book is available from the British Library.

ISBN: PB: 978-0-5676-7127-1
ePDF: 978-0-5676-7128-8
ePub: 978-0-5676-7130-1

Library of Congress Cataloging-in-Publication Data
A catalog record for this book is available from the Library of Congress.

Series: T&T Clark Study Guides to the New Testament, volume 13

Cover design: clareturner.co.uk

Typeset by Newgen Knowledge Works (P) Ltd., Chennai, India

CONTENTS

PREFACE AND ACKNOWLEDGEMENTS

In keeping with the Sheffield Phoenix Guides to the New Testament series, this book does not seek to cover in any detail all that might be said about 1 and 2 Thessalonians. Instead, it attempts to narrate the story of the founding of the Christ group in the ancient Roman city of Thessalonike and how the two letters in the canon reflect the continuation of the relationship between that group and what I will call the 'Paul party'. I attempt to ground this narrative in the most up-to-date scholarly work on critical matters of interpretation while also presenting a readable construction that reflects my own best estimates of the situation. Although I try to keep the references to a minimum, I do indicate where interested parties might look for the scholarly research on given topics and reconstructions.

My own research on 1 and 2 Thessalonians from the time of my doctoral dissertation to the present has informed this book. Much of this research has been undertaken with the support of grants from the Social Sciences and Humanities Research Council of Canada. I have presented and published the results in various formats and I am grateful for all the verbal and written feedback I have received along the way. The content of this Guide reflects and builds upon my previously published work in various parts of Chapter 1 (Ascough 2000; 2003), Chapter 2 (Ascough 2009b), Chapter 3 (Ascough 2014), Chapter 4 (Ascough 2004; 2011a), Chapter 5 (Ascough 2009c), and Chapter 6 (Ascough 2010). These publications provide much of the technical argumentation for the construction depicted of the founding and development of the Christ group at Thessalonike. I make reference to a number of texts from ancient associations using the following two abbreviations: *AGRW* = Ascough, Harland, and Kloppenborg 2012 and *GRA* I = Kloppenborg and Ascough 2011. All biblical quotations are from the New Revised Standard Version (NRSV) unless otherwise noted.

I am particularly thankful to the Series editor, Tat-siong Benny Liew, for his fortitude. The acceptance of administrative tasks delayed writing the book longer than I initially hoped, but Benny remained patient with me. My administrative assistants, Cheryl O'Shea and Linda Thomas, were tolerant as I procrastinated on some tasks in order to carve out time to write. Cheryl was particularly helpful in proofreading the entire manuscript. My family has been, as always, longsuffering, as I have disappeared into my office for untold hours to work on this and related projects, even forgoing a summer family vacation along the way. I dedicate this work with love to Mary-Lynne, Hannah and Josiah as a small thanksgiving for their unwavering support for all that I do.

Richard S. Ascough
Summer 2013

ABBREVIATIONS

AB	Anchor Bible
AGRW	Richard S. Ascough, Philip A. Harland, and John S. Kloppenborg, *Associations in the Greco-Roman World: A Sourcebook* (Waco, TX: Baylor University Press, 2012).
ANRW	*Aufstieg und Niedergang der römischen Welt*
ANTC	Abingdon New Testament Commentaries
AWOL	Absent without leave
BBR	*Bulletin for Biblical Research*
BCE	Before the Common Era
BETL	Bibliotheca ephemeridum theologicarum lovaniensium
BibRes	*Biblical Research*
BNTC	Black's New Testament Commentaries
BWANT	Beiträge zur Wissenschaft vom Neuen Testament
BZ	*Biblische Zeitschrift*
CB	Coniectanae biblica
CBQ	*Catholic Biblical Quarterly*
CE	Common Era
CEV	Contemporary English Version
EBib	Etudes bibliques
ECL	Early Christianity and its Literature
GNT	Good News Today
GRA	John S. Kloppenborg and Richard S. Ascough, *Greco-Roman Associations: Texts, Translations, and Commentary*. I. *Attica, Central Greece, Macedonia, Thrace*, (Beihefte zur Zeitschrift für die neutestamentliche Wissenschaft und die Kunde der älteren Kirche, 181; Berlin and New York: Walter de Gruyter, 2011).
HTR	*Harvard Theological Review*
HTS	Harvard Theological Studies
HUT	Hermeneutische Untersuchungen zur Theologie
HvTSt	*Hervormde teologiese studies*
ICC	International Critical Commentary
Int	*Interpretation*
IVP	InterVarsity Press
JBL	*Journal of Biblical Literature*
JSNT	*Journal for the Study of the New Testament*
JSNTSup	Journal for the Study of the New Testament Supplements
LNTS	Library of New Testament Studies
NICNT	New International Commentary on the New Testament
NIGTC	New International Greek Testament Commentary
NIV	New International Version
NLT	New Living Translation

NovT	*Novum Testamentum*
NRSV	New Revised Standard Version
NTOA	Novum Testamentum et orbis antiquus
NTS	*New Testament Studies*
NTTS	New Testament Tools and Studies
P.Merton	H. Idris Bell and C.H. Roberts *et al.* (eds.), *A Descriptive Catalogue of the Greek Papyri in the Collection of Wilfred Merton* (London: E. Walker, 1948–).
SBLDS	Society of Biblical Literature Dissertation Series
SNTSMS	Society for New Testament Studies Monograph Series
SP	Sacra pagina
STAC	Studien und Texte zu Antike und Christentum
TUGAL	Texte und Untersuchungen zur Geschichte der altchristlichen Literatur
TynBul	*Tyndale Bulletin*
WBC	Word Biblical Commentary
WUNT	Wissenschaftliche Untersuchungen zum Neuen Testament
ZNW	*Zeitschrift für wissenschaftliche Theologie*

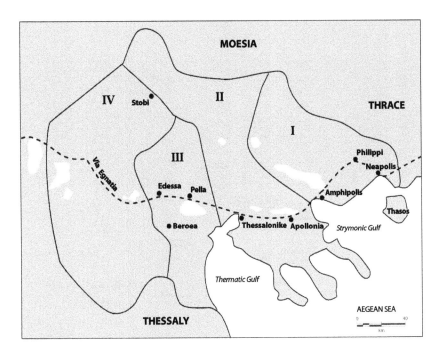

Map 1. Map of Macedonia with Districts and the *Via Egnatia*

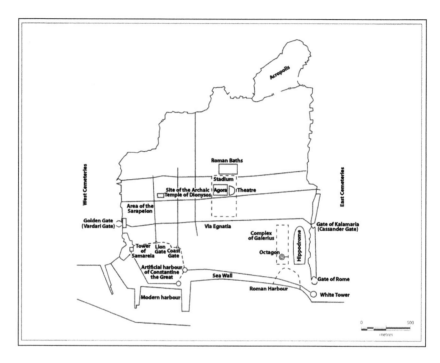

West Cemeteries

East Cemeteries

Acropolis

Roman Baths

Stadium

Site of the Archaic
Temple of Dionysos

Agora

Theatre

Area of the
Sarapeion

Golden Gate
(Vardari Gate)

Via Egnatia

Gate of Kalamaria
(Cassander Gate)

Complex
of Galerius

Tower
of
Samareia

Lion
Gate

Coast
Gate

Octagon

Hippodrome

Artificial harbour
of Constantine
the Great

Sea Wall

Gate of Rome

Roman Harbour

White Tower

Modern harbour

0   500

metres

Map 2. Map of Thessalonike with Roman and Byzantine Monuments

Introduction

The two canonical letters addressed to Christ adherents living in Thessalonike are among the shortest of the letters attributed to Paul. The first of these letters—1 Thessalonians—is thought by many scholars to be one of the earliest extant letters written by Paul. Whether or not Paul wrote 2 Thessalonians, on the other hand, remains a point of debate among scholars. Nevertheless, everything that we know about the first generation or two of Christ adherents in this cosmopolitan city stems from these two letters, along with a brief passage in the Book of Acts and a few comments scattered in other of Paul's letters. This is not very much information on which to construct a picture of the organization, practices and beliefs of the Christ group, or groups, at Thessalonike. Nevertheless, through the judicious application of different methods, biblical scholars have been able to piece together an understanding of some of the primary social and theological aspects of the Thessalonian believers.

Archaeological work on Thessalonike, while not very extensive, has helped us develop an understanding of the types of people who lived in the city and how they were organized both politically and socially. Just as useful in this regard are descriptions of the city in non-biblical writings from the first century of the Common Era. At the same time, study of ancient letter writing practices has given us insight into the nature of Pauline letters, sometimes helping us uncover the goals for writing these letters. Studies of ancient rhetoric—the art of persuasion—have helped us see how letter writers use language to persuade audiences. From such literary study we are able to establish what a writer thinks about particular issues.

At the same time, we can 'mirror-read' the text to determine what are the concerns of the recipients of a letter—their actions, their concerns and their questions. That said, such a strategy must be used with caution, since we really only have the point of view of the letter writers, and they may not fully, or even accurately, depict the situation of the audience to which they write. Mirror-reading may also become somewhat circular, insofar as once mirror-reading is used to construct a particular picture of the audience, that picture can then be used to affirm particular readings of texts. Nevertheless, used cautiously, we can use the strategy to gain a preliminary sense of concerns that the writers highlight, and perhaps get some idea of where they disagree with the practices and beliefs of an audience insofar as the letters convey attempts to correct them. Unfortunately, we rarely know whether Paul and his co-writers were successful in this persuasion—whether or not the audience actually shifted their beliefs and practices. All the letters provide is a snapshot in time of particular communities.

This brings us to the nature of this introductory book—it is a 'snapshot' of the Thessalonian Christ believers during Paul's time, as constructed from the letters they received. Yet due to the controversial nature of many conclusions drawn from Paul's two letters to the Thessalonians, rather than think of the book as a single snapshot, it is perhaps better to imagine it as a set of snapshots. As we explore the two letters we will discuss various theories that scholars have about the content and structure of the letters themselves and the nature of the community to which Paul and his companions write. Each scholarly theory is important, although since some theories are contradictory, not all of them are correct. As an analogy, and in keeping with the 'snapshot' metaphor, it is perhaps helpful to think of the work of biblical scholarship as akin to using a computer program to adjust a picture. We all begin with somewhat the same blurry image, but each scholar sharpens the image, adjusts the colour and trims the edges somewhat differently. As a result, different pictures emerge, although all of them do have some vague resemblance to the 'original'. In biblical studies, however, we do not have an 'original' with which to compare our own versions of the picture. All we can do is continue to compare and contrast different constructed pictures to determine which of them seem to be more authentic and which seem to be lacking in some crucial way.

As we move through this introductory book we will be highlighting the various constructions that scholars have offered about the many interesting aspects of 1 and 2 Thessalonians and the community to which they are addressed. I will note the relative strengths and weaknesses of the images, and give some indication why one particular picture is to be preferred over the others, all the while keeping in mind that these pictures will still need further refinement. Although I try to be fair, I do, of course, have my views on the founding and structure of the Thessalonian Christ group and the meaning of the two letters written to them. It is perhaps inevitable that my own views will dominate the overall picture here, often reflecting the more detailed, technical papers I have published on the Thessalonian letters (see entries in the Bibliography).

Before turning to modern scholarly attempts to reconstruct the origins and development of the Thessalonian Christ group, it seems appropriate to begin with what is likely the very first attempt to construct a composite picture of the Jesus believing community at Thessalonike at their very earliest point. The writer of the Book of Acts sought to narrate the spread of the message of Jesus from Jerusalem to Rome, and provides a number of his own snapshots along the way. There is now widespread agreement that not every detail the writer provides is necessarily historically accurate according to modern conventions of history. That said, very few scholars think that the writer simply invented everything in Acts. Rather, the Book of Acts has its own agenda, and in pursuing that agenda, the writer gives us some snippets of information about the formation of various communities of believers. In the case of Thessalonike, the writer provides only a single episode of substance about the believers there:

> After Paul and Silas had passed through Amphipolis and Apollonia, they came to Thessalonica, where there was a synagogue of the Jews. And Paul went in, as was his custom, and on three Sabbath days argued with them from the scriptures, explaining and proving that it was necessary for the Messiah to suffer and to rise from the dead, and saying, 'This is the Messiah, Jesus whom I am proclaiming to you'. Some of them were persuaded and joined Paul and Silas, as did a great many of the devout Greeks and not a few of the leading women. But the Jews became jealous, and with the help of some ruffians in the marketplaces they formed a mob and set the city in an uproar. While they were searching for Paul and Silas to bring them out to the assembly, they attacked Jason's house. When they could not find them, they dragged Jason and some believers before the city authorities, shouting, 'These people who have been turning the world upside down have come here also, and Jason has entertained them as guests. They are all acting contrary to the decrees of the emperor, saying that there is another king named Jesus.' The people and the city officials were disturbed when they heard this, and after they had taken bail from Jason and the others, they let them go. That very night the believers sent Paul and Silas off to Beroea (Acts 17.1-10a).

Once Paul and Silas departed Thessalonike, they continued to travel and establish new Christ groups throughout the northeastern areas of the circum-Mediterranean. Their first letter to the Thessalonians—at least the first letter that has survived—seems to date from sometime around 49–51 CE. The content of the letter, particularly their attempts in 1 Thessalonians 2 to placate the Thessalonian believers who were taken aback by their rather hasty departure, would suggest that the time between the initial visit and letter was close, perhaps a matter of weeks. At the same time, that the Thessalonians are concerned about 'those who have died' (4.13) would suggest that some time has passed since Paul and his companions' departure, unless we can assume that there was an epidemic that took the lives of a few believers in quick succession (an unlikely conjecture).

According to information we can glean from the letters, it seems likely that Paul and his companions stayed in Thessalonike somewhat longer than the three weeks indicated in Acts. In the letter to the Philippians the writers note that they received money from the Philippians at least twice while they were at Thessalonike (Phil. 4.16), presumably to supplement the income they were earning through working with their hands (1 Thess. 2.9; 4.11).

Although we do not know quite how long Paul and the others were in Thessalonike, it was clearly long enough to establish a group. Once they left the city, they remained in contact with the Thessalonian Christ group by sending Timothy from Athens (1 Thess. 3.1-2). When Timothy returned to Paul, he brought news of the Thessalonian believers, including some specific questions and concerns. A letter from the Thessalonians may well have supplemented Timothy's oral report. Malherbe (1990) argues that although there is no explicit mention in 1 Thessalonians of such a letter from the Thessalonian Christ group, the writers' use of epistolographic clichés in describing Timothy's work makes it likely that Timothy brought with him to Thessalonike a (now lost) letter from the Paul party to which the Thessalonians responded with a (now lost) letter of their own in which they raised some issues and questions. Whether oral, written or some combination thereof, the responses of Paul, Silvanus and Timothy to these issues form the substance of 1 Thessalonians.

It is a well-recognized axiom in biblical scholarship that while the Book of Acts can tell us much about the theological and social concerns of its writer, when it comes to information about Paul and other early followers of Jesus it is, at best, a secondary source and must be used with caution. The letters, on the other hand, at least the ones considered 'authentic', are treated as firsthand accounts of historical interchanges between Paul and his companions and the groups they founded. Thus, we must always turn first to the letters themselves for information about the different Christ groups, using Acts only to supplement the picture that emerges, and even then only cautiously.

In the following pages we will begin with a description of the founding of the Christ group at Thessalonike (Chapter 1), drawing primarily on the text of 1 Thessalonians and information gleaned from archaeological data here and elsewhere. Due to the scant detailed information, however, we will also draw upon a composite picture of typical group behaviours among small, unofficial groups in various urban centres in the Greek and Roman period. These associations will be described in Chapter 1 as they help us construct a picture of Paul's work among the Thessalonians. Once Paul and his companions founded the Christ group at Thessalonike, they left the city but, as we noted above, remained in contact, including the sending of a letter in response to receiving a report about the Thessalonian Christ group. In Chapter 2 we will look at the nature of letter writing in antiquity and extrapolate some details about the composition of 1 Thessalonians.

In antiquity, as with today, correspondence of various types (back then, letters; today, texting, tweets and emails) aimed to maintain and build relationships among people. In Chapter 3 we will examine how this relationship developed after the departure of Paul's party from the city. It seems that the Thessalonian Christ group's reputation spread even as they themselves worried over why Paul needed to depart. The letter writers assure the Thessalonians that their local leadership is sufficient to guide them and should be honoured appropriately. Much of the body of 1 Thessalonians focuses on this relationship building by responding to specific requests for guidance that Timothy had brought following his visit to Thessalonike. In Chapter 4 we will note how Paul and his co-writers affirm the Thessalonians in their commitment to God, urging them to remain pure with regard to sexual morality, quiet in their work habits and hopeful in the face of the death of some of their compatriots.

As time moves along, communities rarely remain static; rather, they adjust and adapt to new circumstances and developing ideas and theologies. The letter called '2 Thessalonians' reflects just such a community adaptation, so much so that according to many, albeit not all, scholars, it is not likely to have been written during Paul's lifetime. In Chapter 5 we will look at why some scholars argue that this letter is a post-Pauline composition, and the arguments that are used to counter this view. Although far from solved to everyone's liking, in order to move forward from this debate we must take a side, and in this case my own view is that 2 Thessalonians was written to the same Christ group as 1 Thessalonians, but by an anonymous author or authors who used the name of Paul in order to lend authority to the letter. Far from being duplicitous, this practice—called pseudonymity— was common enough in antiquity, and this little letter is not likely to be the only one in the Bible written in the name of a famous person. The decision to place it later rests on a number of factors that we shall explore, but for now we can highlight that if we are correct in this, a careful reading of the letter will give us a glimpse into how the Christ group developed into the second generation of adherents. There is continuity, certainly, but there is also a greater concern with regulating behaviours within the group, as we shall explore in the latter part of Chapter 6. In the Epilogue we will look briefly at community developments in the following centuries and the place of the letters in the canonical process.

Our intent in this introductory book is not to offer a full verse-by-verse commentary of 1 and 2 Thessalonians, so many verses will be left aside. Rather, we hope to present an overview of the historical development of the Christ group at Thessalonike while demonstrating how these two letters inform the historians' craft of (re)constructing social structures and theological developments. As such, the book is not meant to be an ending point, drawing together a variety of pieces to present one grand narrative. Rather, it should be read as an invitation to enter into the discussion about the origins and development of one of the many fascinating communities of Christ adherents founded by Paul and others in the first century of the Common Era.

FOUNDING A CHRIST GROUP AT THESSALONIKE

The Paul Party Comes to Town

We can imagine that it was a dry, dusty summer day when a ragtag band arrived in Thessalonike on foot, entering through the eastern gate on the *Via Egnatia*. The 153 kilometres from Philippi would take at least a week of walking five or more hours a day on the well-maintained Roman thoroughfare. Along the way they perhaps stayed a night or two at Amphipolis and again at Apollonia (Acts 17.1). While out on the road, they would inevitably meet up with many different sorts of travellers moving both east and west: merchants carting their wares, pilgrims going to or returning from a sacred site, slaves carrying messages for their masters, Roman soldiers moving from one area to another. At the appearance of this latter group everyone made way, hoping that they would not be called upon to carry some soldier's pack for a mile or so. Among this ragtag band at least three are known by name: Paul, Silvanus and Timothy. They were heading eastward to establish yet another urban group that would be devoted to Christ. They had been on the road for some time, with successes and failures in the major urban centres of the eastern empire. As they entered into the bustle of the capital city of the Roman province of Macedonia they looked forward to a cool glass of water as their minds turned to where they would spend their first night.

All of this is, of course, conjectural. Perhaps it was a cold, damp winter's day, or perhaps the travellers rode on a donkey or in a cart. Yet whenever we hear that 'Paul came to Thessalonike' all of us, consciously or more likely not, have some notion of how he made his arrival. Likewise, when we claim 'Paul founded the Thessalonian Christ group' we invoke an imaginative process about what took place. The historian's task is to fill in as many gaps as possible, using the best available evidence. It will, of necessity, always remain conjectural, for we can never know all the details with certainty, even if we did have first-hand accounts (which we do not in this particular case). The historian marshals the evidence to present a plausible case for what took place. At the very least, it must be consistent with the available evidence. In the description above, the time of year was chosen arbitrarily, but the types of travellers one might meet on the *Via Egnatia*, the main east-west thoroughfare through the Roman province of Macedonia, is consistent with multiple first- and second-hand accounts of travel in Roman antiquity. Thus, it is a plausible, if not entirely provable, depiction of the arrival of Paul and his colleagues in Thessalonike.

In this chapter we will continue in the same vein, making suggestions about what took place in the founding of the Christ group at Thessalonike, making note of the available evidence whenever possible. This depiction is quite different in places from the truncated account in Acts, and reasons for these differences will be noted, along with some of the similarities. The fact of the matter is that there are details in the Acts account that seem to contradict facts we know about the Christ group at Thessalonike, and at the very least these must be explained. And so, we return to our narrative, taking up the story of our dishevelled travellers as they arrive at the city.

Entering the city through the Kassandreia Gate, they could see the *Via Egnatia* continue in a straight line towards the centre of town, where they assumed it would pass through the main marketplace—the forum—and continue to the western wall where there would be another gate much like the one they had just passed (the 'Golden' gate). Unlike many Greek cities that have the curved and sometimes meandering streets that reflect the ancient goat paths that were at their very foundations, Thessalonike is decidedly Roman in its design. Kassander, a general who served under Alexander the Great, founded the city in 315 BCE, probably on or near the site of a town called Thermae. Kassander named it after his wife, Thessalonika, the stepsister of Alexander (Strabo, *Geography* 7, Frg. 24). In 167 CE, the Romans made Thessalonike the capital of the second district of Macedonia and thus the seat of a Roman governor, and two decades later it became the capital of the entire province when the Romans reorganized the district boundaries in 146 BCE. This promotion greatly enhanced the city's power and stature By the mid-first century, Thessalonike had a bustling population of 40,000 or more (de Vos 1999: 129; cf. vom Brocke 2001: 72, whose estimates seem somewhat on the low side; vom Brocke 2001 provides a detailed survey of the history, development, economy and society of Thessalonike from Hellenistic through Roman times, but is only available in German).

Thessalonike had long been a fortified city when the Romans arrived in 168 BCE, and these fortifications were incorporated into the expanded Roman walls. In the late Republican period many Romans had settled in the city and it grew so much that many public and private buildings stood outside its walls, which had fallen into disrepair. Thessalonike's refusal to back Brutus and Cassius, the assassins of Julius Caesar, was rewarded after the battle of Philippi (42 CE). Thessalonike was proclaimed a free city and rebuilding undertaken. The walls were extended and refortified, and the streets were reworked to run perpendicular in a north-south and east-west direction. This made navigation of the streets easy, aided by the fact that some of these streets were given numerical designations such as 'Twelfth Street' (see *AGRW* 55; for details on Roman town planning in Thessalonike, see Adam-Veleni 2003: 134-62).

Within this grid of streets, Paul and his companions finally settled on looking for work in order to provide for their basic needs—food and shelter. Given their skills as artisans, they knew that it would be easy enough to find temporary employment in one of the many small workshops that populated the inner streets of the bustling commercial port centre that was Thessalonike. They gravitated to Eighteenth Street, where they had already heard there was a cluster of small leather workshops alongside ancillary operations, and thus an ideal place to find work. This is the typical pattern in cities across the Roman Empire. Workshops dealing in the same or similar goods and services would locate near one another, often sharing resources and suppliers even while competing for customers. Given the ebb and flow of demand for their goods, such workshops could employ a small number of permanent staff, usually slaves, and then supplement them with temporary workers when necessary. In 1 Thess. 2.9 the writers recall for the Thessalonians their time together, noting, 'You remember our labor and toil, brothers and sisters; we worked night and day, so that we might not burden any of you while we proclaimed to you the gospel of God' (cf. 2 Thess. 3.8). Later in the letter, the writers will exhort the Thessalonian Christ followers 'to work with your hands' (4.11), confirming that the primary audience for this letter is a group of manual labourers. Thus, there are clear indications that the Paul party was involved in some sort of manual labour during their time in the city, a supposition now held by most commentators on the text (see Hock 1980; Malherbe 1987: 17-20).

That Paul and his companions were artisans is borne out further in light of Acts 18.1-3, which notes that in Corinth Paul met up with Priscilla and Aquila, 'and, because he was of the same trade, he stayed with them, and they worked together—by trade they were tentmakers' (cf. 1 Cor. 4.12, where Paul also mentions working with his hands). While nowhere does it say explicitly that Paul works with leather, the fact that tents were manufactured from leather suggests that while this might have been Paul's specialty, his skills would have allowed him to work with more than just this one type of leather product (Hock 1980: 22-25). Also in favour of supposing Paul worked with leather goods is the fact that the tools of this trade were small and light and easily carried on one's person when one was travelling from place to place and relying upon temporary work for support, as seems to be the case with Paul and his companions. Finally, as a member of the Pharisee party (Phil. 3.5), Paul would not only have learned to interpret Torah, he would have been required to learn a skilled trade. The only evidence we have points to something that involves handwork, portability and perhaps leather (tents).

At this point the astute reader will note that the text from Acts 17 concerning Thessalonike, quoted in the Introduction, states that the Paul party went first to the 'synagogue of the Jews' where he spent three weeks arguing about the meaning of Jesus' death. Some of these Jews were persuaded, albeit far from the majority, the latter who turned against the visitors had them driven from the town. Alongside those Jews who did believe were 'a great many of the devout Greeks and not a few of the leading women' (Acts 17.4). The epithet 'devout', in Greek literally 'the worshipping Greeks' (*tōn sebomenōn Hellēnōn*), is taken by most commentators to indicate 'God-fearers', a term given to non-Jews who have adopted the worship of the monotheistic God of the Jews without undergoing some of the ritual markers of full inclusion, such as circumcision. The writer of Acts refers variously to this category of Jewish sympathizers on a few occasions (Acts 10.2, 22; 13.16, 26; 16.4; 17.4, 17; 18.7). In this account, then, it would seem that the first adherents of the Christ group were Jews and monotheistic non-Jews who attended the synagogue.

This does not fit, however, with information contained in 1 Thessalonians, and thus many scholars have discounted the Acts narrative as reflecting that writer's particular understanding of Christianity, which sees it as always and everywhere rooted in its Jewish antecedents. In the case of Thessalonike the writers of the first letter state very clearly that the initial adherents to Christ are known in regions beyond the city for having 'turned to God from idols, to serve a living and true God' (1.9). This is not how anyone would describe a turning away from the Jewish God, for it seems to suggest that the Jewish God was merely an 'idol'. It is certainly not what one would expect from a Pharisee such as Paul. The natural understanding of this text is that these initial adherents in Thessalonike were not Jewish or even Jewish sympathizers. They were, in fact, non-Jews who worshipped one or more of the many deities in the Greek and Roman pantheon, if not also a few local gods alongside them. The Thessalonian Christ group is thus a Gentile group at its core (see further de Vos 1999: 146-47; Ascough 2003: 202-203).

Proclaiming the Message

Picking up our story, Paul, Silvanus and Timothy had now, we assume, found work in a leather shop on one of the industrial streets in the inner city of Thessalonike. As always, the work was physically taxing in less than ideal conditions. Workshops were tough places to earn a living. The type of place the Paul party found was probably similar to the typical small artisan workshops that have been unearthed in Roman urban centres throughout the empire. Cheaply constructed apartment blocks of three to six stories stood on either side of the street. In the one- or two-room residences families made their homes in the upper floors, sleeping side-by-side at night, and moving the bedding aside in the day to make room for other activities. For the most part, the ground floor was turned over to commerce, with businesses often run by the families living above. A wide variety of products were sold in these shops, such as clothing, shoes, jewellery, fabric, spices and baked goods. Customers would purchase wares at the front counter, while those same products were being produced in the back of the open room. Many other shops were run as taverns, fast food outlets or even brothels.

In a leather shop, workers would sit on the floor or at low tables using their tools variously to cut, sew and trim leather to produce whatever goods were in demand—usually sandals, outer clothing and animal harnesses, although occasionally a Roman official might place a bulk order for military outfits and equipment such as leather shields or tents. In the workshop the men would coordinate their efforts, each taking a specific task for the day to ensure the production line ran smoothly. It was a difficult way of life, with each workday lasting from dawn until dusk. Most workers could earn enough money to feed their family for the day, but little else. As a second-century Roman writer notes, 'Their trades were petty, laborious, and barely able to supply them with just enough' (Lucian, *The Runaways*, 13, LCL). This type of work would take its toll, both physically and psychologically.

Nevertheless, it is not all drab and dire. The men working in such shops did form friendships and relationships (for the most part it was the men who did the work; other industries were dominated by women, but there were few places where there was intermixing of the genders). We know about these friendships and relationships through inscriptions that were erected in antiquity. In fact, in many cases, workers in shops such as the one in which the Paul party found work would organize themselves into guilds. Unlike today's unions, such guilds had very little economic power; they could not go on strike or bargain for higher wages. They could, however, organize and engage in mutually beneficial social activities. And judging from the inscriptions they set up, they did a lot of socializing, often holding banquets or drinking parties. The paucity of archeological evidence from Thessalonike noted above means we do not have a lot of information from this particular city, but there is no reason to think it was different from cities elsewhere in the empire in which there is ample evidence for the activities of such groups. Nevertheless, there are at least sixteen identifiable association inscriptions from first- and early second-century Thessalonike. The following are representative inscriptions set up by associations in the city:

> For Aulus Papius Chilon who established the meeting place (*oikos*). The sacred object-bearers and fellow-banqueters: [*twelve names follow, concluding with that of the leader*] (*AGRW* 47, first century BCE–first century CE).

Year 214. Herennia Procula, fulfilling the promise of her father Marcus Herennius Proculus, has set up for the fellow-banqueters four columns with capitals and bases as well as the lintel, during the priesthood of Leonidas son of Lysanias (*AGRW* 48, 66–67 CE).

This is dedicated to Theos Hypsistos ('Highest God') on behalf of Titus Flavius Euktimenos son of Amuntas, head of the banquet, by the fellow-banqueters recorded below: [*a list of 38 male names follows*] (*AGRW* 51, late first century CE).

These associations were clearly formed in order for the members to spend time eating and drinking together.

Such parties were costly affairs and beyond the wages of the association members, so in many cases the association would find a patron—a person of wealth and privilege who would give them money for their social activities. These patrons did not demand repayment. They did, however, expect to be thanked, often in quite public and grandiose ways. As a result, many groups set up inscriptions honouring their patrons, such as this:

Marcus Minatius son of Sextus, Roman, is a noble and good man, acting piously towards the gods and glory-loving in relation to the association, displaying love of glory both to individuals and to the association…. Furthermore, he also invited all of us to the sacrifice, which he prepared for the gods to be accomplished for the association, and he invited us to the banquet (*AGRW* 224, Delos, 153/152 BCE).

Although social activities were a way for group members to live life to the fullest, as is the case with all human beings, life must eventually come to an end. And like people throughout history, the Romans were sometimes curious, often fearful, about what happens to a person after death. Part of that worry was expressed in a concern for a proper, decent burial. But funerals cost money, which was lacking among the labourers of the time. In many instances, however, membership in an association could have an added benefit of the promise of a proper burial, funded by the association itself, perhaps from membership dues but more likely from the largesse of patrons and benefactors. Thus, many associations set up inscriptions to commemorate their departed members, such as this one from Thessalonike:

When Gaius Autronius Liberus, also called Glykon, was head of the synagogue (*archisynagōgos*), Quintus Papius Castor was secretary, and Hermogenes son of Diogenes was accountant, the association of Aphrodite Epiteuxidia set this up as a memorial for Athenion son of Praxiteles, who has died outside of Amastris. This was set up through their supervisors. Farewell! So also will you be sometime! Year 122 (*AGRW* 49, 90–91 CE).

Given the pattern of group formation among artisan workers that is evident from the inscriptions that have been and continue to be found from the Greek and Roman period, it is most probable that the workers that Paul and

his companions had joined in the workshop had an established guild structure that facilitated their social activities. One might expect that each day
the workshop was not just abuzz with activity but was humming with chat-
ter among the workers. Given the long shifts, conversations would cover
recent news events, local gossip, retelling of tales of past exploits, arguments over sports, boasting of sexual exploits and any number of other
topics, not unlike workplaces in our own time. Among the topics sure to
come up would be the role of the gods, for very little was done in the ancient
world without some invocation of the gods. Each man in the shop would be
familiar with many of the Roman and Greek gods, as well as some of the
local Macedonian or Thessalonian gods such as Theos Hypsistos or Cabirus
(see Edson 1948; Donfried 1985) or the Dioscuri (divine twins) Castor and
Polydeuces, known through the civic cults of Thessalonike (Kloppenborg
1993), or even some recent imports such as Isis and Sarapis (Steimle 2008:
79-131; Koester 2010).

Unlike today in the Western world where we might inquire as to whether
someone 'believes' in a god, in the Roman world the existence of the gods
were taken for granted. In general the gods were just as much a part of the
fabric of life as the air. While not necessarily malevolent, they were capri-
cious and if a person paid attention to the gods it was generally to ensure
that they did not elicit their undue attention, for the gods could be mean.
Nevertheless, at times one might appeal to the gods for good fortune and
blessings in life.

Within the workshop setting, a workers' association would have a patron
deity to whom they especially looked for favours, perhaps invoking them
for a productive day or pouring out a libation in their honour at a banquet.
Paul and his companions would be acutely aware of such practices, noting
the name and nature of the god chosen by the workers of their adopted
workplace. When the writers of 1 Thessalonians recall 'we worked night
and day…while we proclaimed to you the gospel of God' (2.9), we should
not imagine that they stood upon a stool and proclaimed aloud a sermon
calling for conversion. The image presented in the text is much more subtle;
these men worked with their hands, engaging their colleagues in conversation over the course of the day, likely turning the discussion to the nature of
the gods whenever they could.

It must have taken quite some resolve to raise these issues with their co-
workers in the shop. As a result of their last major effort to found a Christ
group they had suffered and been shamefully treated in the city of Philippi
(1 Thess. 2.2). It may be that they had been thrown in jail for their speaking
about Christ (as narrated in Acts 16.23-24), but at the very least it seems that
they had been subjected to verbal and physical abuse for their efforts. And
as they indicate in their letter to the Thessalonians, such was also the case
in the workshop. They note that they 'had courage in our God to declare to

you the gospel of God in the face of great opposition' (2.2). Yet converse they did, and, it seems, not without success.

Realigning the Group

One can imagine the laughter and jeering, and perhaps even outright hostility, which took place when Paul, Silvanus and Timothy conveyed details about their belief in Christ. When Paul first broached the subject of religion there was probably some interest among the other workers in the shop. By the mid-first century many foreign deities had migrated to take up residence in various Roman cities. Some of those in the workshop might already have heard about the God of Judea and were perhaps curious about what this God might have to offer them. The approach to religion at the time was quite utilitarian, reckoning the difference between what the god would provide versus what it would cost to align oneself with the god. A god that promised much, such as safety and success and perhaps a few extra banquet days, and demanded little by way of cult activities such as libations and sacrifices, could prove attractive to many. On the other hand, a god that required a lot of maintenance was not likely to draw big crowds unless there was something worthwhile at stake.

Although we do not know a lot about how new deities were introduced and took root in ancient cities, there is a particularly interesting example that is narrated on an inscription found at Thessalonike. The story revolves around establishing the cult of Sarapis in the town of Opus, in the central Greece region of Lokris. The story took place in the second century BCE, although the inscription itself came from first-century CE Thessalonike, suggesting that the story continued to circulate not only in Opus but also in Thessalonike. The initial dream in the story takes place in the Sarapeum in Thessalonike, which is where the inscription was found in 1921.

> …during the embassy…to enter into the shrine (*oikos*), it seemed in his sleep that Sarapis stood beside him and told him that after having arrived in Opus, he should carry a message to Eurynomos son of Timasitheos to receive Sarapis and his sister Isis, and that he should deliver to him [Eurynomos] the letter under the pillow. And waking up, he [Xenainetos] marveled at the dream and yet he was at a loss about what he should do because he was a political rival to Eurynomos. But, falling asleep again, and seeing the same things, when he awoke he found the letter under the pillow, just as it had been indicated to him. Now when he had returned [to Opus], he gave the letter to Eurynomos and reported the things that were decreed by the god. Now when Eurynomos received the letter and heard the things that Xenainetos said, he was at a loss because they were political rivals towards one other, as was made clear above. After having read the letter and having seen that the things that were written were in agreement with the things first having been said by him [Xenainetos], he [Eurynomos] received Sarapis and Isis. After he provided

> hospitality in the household (*oikos*) of Sosinike, she received Sarapis and
> Isis among the household gods. Sosinike offered the sacrifices for a certain
> time. And after her death Eunosta, the granddaughter of Sosibas, when she
> received the office, administered the mysteries of the gods among those not
> initiated into the sacred rites. When Eunosta finally fell ill…sacrificed on her
> behalf… (*AGRW* 52, first century–second century CE; for commentary on
> this text see *GRA* I 77).

Unfortunately, the bottom portion of inscription is broken, so we do not
know how the story concludes. There are a number of interesting features
in what we can read. First and foremost, we can see that one of the great
attractions of the Egyptian god Sarapis was his ability to communicate with
mortals through letters and dreams. He also brokered the reconciliation of
two rivals in Opus when he asked them to bring him into the town. Sarapis
brought with him his sister Isis, but their requirements were not great; they
were content, it seems, with a household shrine, around which, presumably,
a small group of devotees gathered regularly, led by a priestess. When the
inscription breaks off, we can see that already there had been two or three
generations of priestesses, suggesting that the Sarapis cult was an ongoing
concern in the town of Opus.

In contrast, the God that Paul and his companions wanted to introduce
to the Thessalonians must have seemed very demanding. For the most part,
new gods were content to reside alongside the other family, civic or national
deities, accepting the offerings of devotees in peaceful co-existence with
other gods. Paul's God would have none of that! This God demanded nothing less than full and exclusive commitment. This is the nature of what
scholars term 'monotheism', in contrast to 'polytheism'. The latter term
indicates that many ('poly') deities ('theism') can be worshipped together
by the same person or group. The word 'mono' indicates 'only' or 'alone'.
This is the central tenant of worshipping the Jewish deity, articulated in
many places throughout the Hebrew sacred texts, such as:

> I am the LORD your God, who brought you out of the land of Egypt, out of
> the house of slavery; you shall have no other gods before me. You shall not
> make for yourself an idol, whether in the form of anything that is in heaven
> above, or that is on the earth beneath, or that is in the water under the earth.
> You shall not bow down to them or worship them; for I the LORD your
> God am a jealous God, punishing children for the iniquity of parents, to the
> third and the fourth generation of those who reject me, but showing stead-
> fast love to the thousandth generation of those who love me and keep my
> commandments (Exod. 20.2-6; cf. Deut. 5.6-10).

This exclusivity would have rattled the Paul party's audience. The recognition of one single god at the expense of others was, in the ancient world,
akin to atheism. It was a denial of the full range of the gods. From a practical point of view, it was, to invoke a modern phrase, 'putting all one's eggs

in a single basket'. By ignoring the other gods one ran the risk of alienating them or even inciting their wrath. Things might start to go badly if this new deity turned out not to be all that powerful, and the old deities took their revenge upon those who ignored them. In the context of the workshop, this revenge might manifest itself in workplace accidents, or the drying up of the supply of raw goods for manufacturing, or a drop in sales, or any number of other calamities. There was much at stake in keeping the regular gods happy.

Unfortunately, 1 Thessalonians does not narrate how the shop workers reached a decision to align themselves with the God of Jesus; it only tells us that they did so: 'you turned to God from idols, to serve a living and true God' (1 Thess. 1.9). They must have become convinced by the arguments of the Paul party that the gods they feared and worshipped were not gods at all, merely 'idols' who had no power. In contrast, the God about which Paul spoke was real and would recognize their allegiance in some good way. There is no question that such convincing would have taken quite some time.

The use of 'you' in 1.9 is interesting insofar as it can be read in two ways. In Greek the word is the plural pronoun and as such could suggest that it means a collection of individuals. In this regard it could mean that a number of persons came to agree with Paul and his companions of their own accord. On the other hand, the plural 'you' could also indicate collective action, as in 'all of you together'. The former understanding is typical among interpreters as it fits with a modern sense of individualism and the right of each person to choose his or her own religion. This reflects our own culture, however, and not that of Roman antiquity, which was a 'collectivist' culture. As such, people were 'group-oriented' and unlikely to adopt a new view unless the viewpoint of the group as a whole shifted (see Malina 2003: 45; cf. Ascough 2009a: 8-12 for an overview of differences between individualist and collectivist culture). As I imagine it, after a period of intense discussion and debate with Paul and his companions, an already well-established occupational association comprised of the workers in the shop made the *collective* decision to change their primary allegiance. The group would no longer look to their former god or gods for help and protection, nor honour them at their banquets. From this point they would align themselves with the God of Christ alone.

The next verse might give us some indication as to why they made this choice: 'to wait for his Son from heaven, whom he raised from the dead—Jesus, who rescues us from the wrath that is coming' (1.10). Many, albeit not all, scholars think that this verse represents at least part of what was at the heart of the Paul party's preaching in Thessalonike. Although brief, it is grounded in the long history of Jewish apocalyptic thinking and writing that has its origins more than three centuries before the time of Paul.

Apocalyptic literature flourished between 200 BCE and 200 CE, but goes back to the fourth or fifth century BCE. Although in popular terminology today, an 'apocalypse' is a catastrophic event (e.g. nuclear holocaust), this only partially reflects the full import of the Greek word *apokalypsis*. At its root, the word suggests an 'uncovering' or 'disclosure', hence the title 'Revelation' for the last book of the New Testament, in which the seer receives a number of visions of things present and things to come.

Apocalyptic writing and preaching involved interpreting the 'present, earthly circumstances in light of the supernatural world and of the future, and to influence both the understanding and the behaviour of the audience by means of divine authority' (Yarbro Collins 1986: 7). In the case of the Thessalonians, it seems that the Paul party presented a scenario in which they noted the imminent coming of God's emissary—Jesus—back to earth to inaugurate a time of punishment on those not adhering to God and bring reward to those who do. This has implications for how we understand a section of 1 Thessalonians in which the writers respond to concerns about members of the group that have already died, a topic we will explore in Chapter 4. For now, we might surmise that one of the key aspects of the Paul party's message that brought about a new allegiance for the artisans with whom they worked was the imminent danger of God's wrath, and the promise of escape for those who changed their allegiance to the 'living and true God'.

The foregoing picture reflects but one of a few scenarios put forth by scholars concerning how Paul and his companions established the Christ group in the city of Thessalonike (worked out in technical detail in Ascough 2000; cf. Jewett 1993). It certainly is much different than imagining Paul preaching on a street corner or going door-to-door to spread the message. Whether or not all the imaginative details are correct, when scholars turn to the content of 1 Thessalonians itself, there is general agreement that the primary locus of the Christ group was the workshop and that Paul and the others worked alongside the early adherents of the group, most if not all of whom were not Jewish. Some scholars maintain that there must be something to the account in the Book of Acts of Paul visiting a synagogue and, thus, posit a large group of Gentile God-fearers at the core of the Thessalonian Christ group (Laub 1976; Blumenthal 2005). More often, however, there is recognition that the Acts narrative reflects the theological and historical biases of its author (Lührmann 1990; Coulot 2006). That said, there is some coherence between the picture narrated above and the account in Acts. Justin Hardin (2006) has argued that the story in Acts 17 of Jason being arrested for hosting a Christ group in his house presents the accusations brought against him as predicated on the Roman laws banning certain kinds of association meetings. That is, even the writer of Acts presents the core of the Thessalonian Christ group as an association.

Once the church was formed, Paul and his companions continued to work 'night and day' to support themselves (2.9). Occasionally their earnings were supplemented by money sent from the Philippian church: 'For even in Thessalonica you sent me help once and again' (Phil. 4.16). The Paul party might have eventually met with some kind of resistance; they did seem to have left Thessalonica in a hurry, prompting the writers' later assurances in 1 Thessalonians 2 that they were not charlatans. This letter itself indicates an ongoing relationship even after their departure. It is to the nature and content of the letter to which we will turn our attention in the next two chapters.

Written Communication—1 Thessalonians

After having spent time with the Thessalonian Christ believers, getting to know them as they worked alongside them, the Paul party had to leave the city rather suddenly. Although the circumstances for this departure were beyond their control, their sudden disappearance would understandably be the cause of some concern among their new friends. The report from Thessalonike that Timothy brought seems to confirm this, so the Paul party's letter affirms their commitment to the Thessalonians and conveys concern for their wellbeing. They encourage the Thessalonians to persevere in their commitment to worship God through Christ. Through the letter the writers address a number of very practical concerns that Timothy reports are troubling the Thessalonians: sexual morality (4.1-8), the nature of brotherly love (4.9-12), the fate of believers who have died before Jesus' return (4.13-18) and signs preceding Jesus' return (5.1-11). Before looking at how their letter addresses these concerns, however, we must first address some basic issues of our own, such as whether or not Paul actually wrote this letter along with issues of the style and persuasive tone of the letter.

Letter Writing and Delivery

In antiquity letters were generally written either on vellum (animal skins) or, more likely in the first century, papyrus (for this and other information on letter writing, see Richards 2005). The letter itself was written on the *recto* of the papyrus sheet, where the fibres ran horizontally. The other side, where the fibres ran vertically, was the *verso*. After a letter was written, it was either rolled or folded into a long, narrow strip, doubled and tied around the middle with a thread of papyrus fibre, then sealed with clay. The name of the person to whom the letter was addressed was written in large letters on this backside of the letter. Further directions could be added, such as the recipient's village or city or specific delivery instructions.

The Roman postal system was very efficient, helped by the extent and excellent condition of the highways, as well as the placement of distance markers and spacing of stations and inns. Initially Augustus organized a relay system of foot messengers in Italy and the west, but he soon revamped the entire system. He introduced relay stations, which provided horses for mounted couriers so that a single messenger could cover the whole distance. Later couriers thundered down the highways in chariots and all other travellers had to give up the right of way. The English word 'post' comes from the Latin *positus*, which means 'fixed' or 'placed' and refers to the fixed posts or stations in the relay system.

This government system was used primarily for military dispatches and confidential and official documents. Private persons did not have access to the official postal system. Instead a number of options were available to them. Private couriers could be employed, although this was open only to the wealthy. The wealthy might also dispatch a trusted slave with a letter. Most people, however, were dependent on travelling businessmen and friends, or passing strangers who happened to be going in the same direction as the letter. This was risky, however, and often letters went undelivered or packages 'disappeared' along the way. Sometimes a letter would list what should be in a package so the contents could be checked before the one who delivered it received their payment.

Composing by Committee (1 Thess. 1.1)

The seventeenth-century Enlightenment changed the nature of scientific enquiry dramatically, affecting many different academic disciples, including biblical studies. Whereas prior generations had assumed the historicity and reliability of biblical texts, in the new era everything was called into question. For biblical scholars this included the authenticity of each of the writings included in the canon of the New Testament. Attempts to disprove the authenticity of 1 Thessalonians reached their peak in the late nineteenth century (see Rigaux 1956: 120-24). In general, however, such attempts to establish the non-Pauline authorship for 1 Thessalonians have not proven persuasive among the majority of scholars. While there are a few sections that remain controversial (see below), on the whole there is widespread acceptance that Paul is responsible for the content and style of the letter. Some scholars continue to argue that non-Pauline peculiarities in the letter indicate a late first or early second-century date (Crüsemann 2010), but overall these have not been accepted. Thus, it is safe to assume that Paul wrote 1 Thessalonians.

Nevertheless, more recent work in socio-rhetorical analysis has raised issues of just what it means to claim Paul as the author. The prevailing picture even today is of Paul sitting alone in a room with an oil-lamp casting a dim light across the rough wooden table on which he rests his hand, weary from scratching out his thoughts in ink on rough papyrus. Rembrandt's iconographic picture is, in part, largely responsible for such images, but so too is our usual way of thinking about authorship. This picture, however, does not cohere well with studies of ancient compositional practices and so we must refine our understanding. The writing of a letter such as 1 Thessalonians more likely was given over to a person professionally trained in the art of written communication. While there is no doubt that Paul was literate, even educated, the level of writing reflected in this and other letters indicates a facility that would require years of continued practice with the exercise books of the time—the *progymnasmata*.

Rather than composing the letter himself, or even dictating it word for word, Paul and the others working with him would have discussed among themselves and with the actual writer the nature of the ideas they wanted to convey. It would then fall to the writer to apply the full range of rhetorical skills to compose a letter that would be persuasive when read aloud to the intended audience. This latter point is key—letters were not intended for private, silent reading (nor were any other writings in antiquity). Although texts were written down for transport and copied for preservation, they were always read aloud—text became oral performance. Although literate persons (often the elite) might read such works aloud to themselves, or have their slave read aloud, for most people written texts would be delivered orally by someone trained in the art of oral communication. In many cases, this was the same person as the writer. Thus, rather than picturing Paul pondering alone his next turn of phrase, we should imagine that Paul and others were together in a room brainstorming ideas and arguing about policies and procedures, while a scribe took notes, mentally and on a wax tablet, that he (for it was most likely a male) would later craft into a rhetorically effective written presentation.

Such collaborative work is reflected in the very opening of 1 Thessalonians: 'Paul, Silvanus, and Timothy, to the church of the Thessalonians in God the Father and the Lord Jesus Christ' (1.1). The letter itself does not claim to come from Paul alone—he names two others who have had a hand in the composition: Silvanus and Timothy. These two companions of Paul are referenced together also in the opening of 2 Thessalonians and in 2 Cor. 1.19. In this latter text Paul makes a clarifying aside to the Corinthians that 'Silvanus and Timothy and I' were the ones who first proclaimed among them 'the Son of God, Jesus Christ'. It seems that this trio had worked as a team in establishing new Christ groups both in Thessalonike and, shortly thereafter, in Corinth.

Silvanus is most certainly the same person referenced in Acts as Silas, the latter name being a Hebrew or Greek form of the Latinized Silvanus. The writer of Acts presents Silas/Silvanus as a key person in establishing Christ groups in various locales in the circum-Mediterranean. He is first mentioned in Acts 15 in a manner that already assumes his leadership in the broader community. After a falling out with Barnabas, Paul chose Silas/Silvanus as his partner, and they struck out for Syria, travelling along the south coast of modern Turkey (Acts 15.40), and eventually into Macedonia, where they established a group in Philippi and then in Thessalonike (Acts 17.4).

Timothy appears more frequently than Silvanus in the Pauline letters and seems to have been a trusted co-worker and emissary over quite a period of time. He is credited as letter co-writer alongside Paul not only in 1 and 2 Thessalonians, but also in 2 Corinthians, Philippians, Philemon, and Colossians. According to Acts, he is a Jew of mixed parentage, who joins with Paul during the latter's visit to his home city of Lystra in Asia Minor (Acts 16.2). His close association with Paul is reflected in his being named as the recipient of two letters from Paul in which Timothy is presumed to have the top leadership role in a Christ group, despite his youth and inexperience. These two 'pastoral letters'—1 and 2 Timothy—are widely thought to be written much after the death of Paul (and presumably also Timothy) but demonstrate the strength of the latter's impact on the collective memory of the developing Christ movement.

Curiously, the writer of Acts does not include Timothy in the founding of the Thessalonike Christ group, but Timothy reappears with Silas/Silvanus shortly thereafter, when the two 'remain behind' in Beroea, eventually rejoining Paul in Athens (17.14-15; 18.5). We should not make too much of Timothy's absence in the account of the founding of the Thessalonike Christ group, as the writer of Acts has been shown to truncate and amalgamate (and perhaps even fabricate) details.

Like Silvanus, Timothy is credited with foundational proclamation in Corinth (2 Cor. 1.19), yet seems also to have had an active go-between role, since Paul mentions numerous occasions in which Timothy is dispatched to deliver messages to and from various Christ groups. One of these occasions includes a return trip to Thessalonike. When Paul, Silvanus and Timothy are in Athens they are worried about the state of affairs of the Thessalonike Christ group, so they dispatch Timothy to pay them a visit (1 Thess. 3.1-2). It is Timothy's recent return bearing 'the good news of your faith and love' and longing to see Paul and Silvanus (3.6) that has precipitated the writing of 1 Thessalonians.

That both Silas and Timothy are presented as equal to Paul in most of 1 Thessalonians and are with Paul in Macedonia according to Acts suggests they were foundational figures in establishing the Thessalonike Christ group. Throughout the letter the plural 'we' is used, only occasionally replaced by the first-person 'I' when Paul gives personal comments. No scribe is mentioned in 1 Thessalonians. Other letters, however, do demonstrate that Paul used secretaries: Romans does include a greeting from the actual writer (16.22) and in other letters Paul adds a personalized greeting in his 'own hand', suggesting that he is not the primary penman for the letter (1 Cor. 16.21; Gal. 6.11; cf. Col. 4.18; 2 Thess. 3.17). Thus, while it may be tempting to say 'Paul writes...', we must always keep in mind that the words before us in the letter are a product of a complex exchange of ideas of which Paul was a key contributor, but not the only one whose ideas are reflected in the final product. In this regard, we will refer to the 'letter writers' (plural) rather than simply ascribing all of the contents to Paul alone (this is also the case for 1–2 Corinthians, Galatians, Philippians, Colossians and Philemon).

In the Introduction we noted that it was not likely that Paul's visit to Thessalonike would have taken place as early in his journeys as the writer of Acts would have us believe—namely, before 40 CE. In 1 Thessalonians 1 Paul refers to 'Macedonia and Achaia' as two separate Roman administrative provinces. Until 44 CE these two areas were considered one region, but Claudius separated them. Thus, Paul is likely writing after 44 CE (Witherington 2006: 73). The most likely time for the initial arrival at Thessalonike, and the follow-up letter a few weeks or months later, is judged by many scholars to be the end of the fourth decade or the early 50s of the Common Era. This dates the letter at least a decade after Paul's sense of God's commission to proclaim a message about the risen Christ, and leaves plenty of time for him to travel through Syria and Asia Minor into the Roman province of Macedonia, where he first visited Philippi and then Thessalonike.

By the time 1 Thessalonians was composed, Paul and his companions had made their way south to Athens (1 Thess. 3.1) and perhaps even had moved on to Corinth (Acts 18.1). The latter city was a travel hub in antiquity, and a good location from which to dispatch and await news from other locales. Certainly the letters to the Corinthians indicate an extended time of interaction with the believers in the city. As noted above, Timothy had travelled to Thessalonike from Athens and returned to Paul and Silvanus shortly after their arrival in Corinth. As Fee notes, 'this can neither be proved nor disproved; it is simply based on—and fits well with—the few historical data at our disposal' (2009: 5). In any event, the news Timothy bore back to a city in the province of Achaia precipitated the writing of the letter we know as 1 Thessalonians. It is to the structure and contents of this letter we now turn.

Receiving the Letter

In our own day and age we have certain features that characterize our letters. Think of the difference in style and tone between writing a cover letter for a job application and writing a letter of complaint. Even more drastically, think of the difference between the style you would use in writing a letter to a friend, the style used if it was sent via email, and composing a text-message to that same friend. Each of these forms of communication has its own style—its own 'genre'. When Paul and his companions wrote letters they did so using the style format of letter writing in their own day. Scholars have reconstructed this format, which they call Hellenistic episto-lary convention (see Roetzel 1998: 51-65). Examining thousands of letters that have been preserved from the Greco-Roman world reveals that most of them followed a basic pattern:

Greetings
Thanksgiving or Blessing
Body
Instruction (often ethical in nature, and thus in Greek called *paraenesis*)
Closing

Here is a short letter from antiquity in which we can see that format (the text in square brackets has, of course, been added):

[*Greetings*:] Chairas to his dearest Dionysius, many greetings and contin-ual health. I was as much delighted at receiving a letter from you as if I had indeed been in my native place; for apart from that we have nothing.

[*Thanksgiving*:] I may dispense with writing to you with a great show of thanks; for it is to those who are not friends that we must give thanks in words. I trust that I may maintain myself in some degree of serenity and be able, if not to give you an equivalent, at least to show some small return for your affection towards me.

[*Body*:] You sent me two prescription-copies, one of the Archagathian, the other of the caustic plaster. The Archagathian is rightly compounded, but the caustic does not include the relative weight of resin. Please tell me of a strong caustic which can safely be used to cauterize the soles (of the feet); for I am in urgent need. As to the dry [?] plaster, you wrote that there are two kinds.

[*No ethical instructions, but practical instruction ends the body*:] Send me the prescription for the resolvent kind; for the four-drug plaster is also dry [?].

[*Closing*:] This letter is sealed with this [?]. Farewell and remember what I have said (*P.Merton* 12, 58 CE, translation by Stowers 1986: 61-62).

Most letters in antiquity were short like the one above, considerably shorter than most of the letters ascribed to Paul (with the exception of Philemon). Nevertheless, longer letters are not unheard of and given the number of issues Paul and his companions were asked to address, or need to address, in the Christ groups to whom they were writing, the lengthy communications they sent are understandable.

When compared to non-biblical ancient letters, it is clear that 1 Thes-salonians, like all of the Pauline letters, contains the primary divisions of ancient letter writing, or 'epistolary conventions': opening greeting, thanks-giving, body and closing. While there is general agreement concerning the identification of the opening being 1.1, considerable debate continues over how best to divide the remainder of the letter, a problem complicated by the presence of the second thanksgiving section at 2.13-16. In general, however, the letter is understood to have the following divisions:

1.1	Letter opening, in which the writers and the recipients are identified.
1.2-10	Thanksgiving section in which the writers highlight the positive aspects of the recipients and wish them well.
2.1-12	The opening section of the body, or a continuation of the thanksgiving section.
2.13-16	Second thanksgiving, possibly an interpolation (see below).
2.17–3.13	The first part of the body of the letter in which the writers discuss recent interactions with the Thessalonians and their hope to see them again.
4.1–5.11	The second part of the body in which the writers respond to specific issues raised by the Thessalonians themselves, including proper sexual conduct (4.1-8), the nature of brotherly love (4.9-12), and the nature and timing of Jesus' return (4.13–5.11).
5.12-22	The *paraenesis*, general exhortations, in this case primarily focused on local leadership issues.
5.23-28	Letter closing, including final greetings.

There were many different types of letters in antiquity, some sent for private reading, some intended as public documents. These ancient letters can generally be classified according to its contents and form, such as family letters, letters of friendship, advice, admonition, rebuke, complaint and so on. Commentators have struggled to determine precisely to which type, if any, 1 Thessalonians conforms. The lengthy section addressing issues raised by the Thessalonians with recommendations and advice (4.1–5.22) has led many commentators to classify 1 Thessalonians as a *paraenetic* letter, one that gives moral exhortation (Malherbe 1989: 49; 1992: 279-93), although Jewett has suggested that it best fits the category of 'praising' or 'thankful' letter in which 'approval is expressed, encouragement is given, and gratitude is shown' (1986: 71). There are some who argue, however, that it includes features of a letter of consolation, which brings comfort and care to the Thessalonians, particularly during their time of separation (Chapa 1994; A. Smith 1995) or features of a letter of friendship, commending the community for their actions (Schoon-Janssen 2000). Both of these types of letters affirm existing good relations between the writers and recipients.

Prior to 1980 there were a number of theories that questioned the literary integrity of 1 Thessalonians, suggesting that it was composed of multiple letter fragments 'pasted' together to form one letter, or that it has one or more sections 'interpolated' or inserted into the authentic letter written by Paul and his companions. With one exception, none of these theories has proved persuasive among scholars and commentators. The exception is Richard, who argues that 1 Thessalonians is a composite of two early letters, both written by Paul to Thessalonike (1995: 11-19). The first letter (2.13–4.2) reviews his time in the city shortly after departure and in light of Timothy's report of his visit. The second letter (1.1–2.12 plus 4.3–5.28) is written later to address specific questions raised by the community, since it reflects a more developed group. It was used to frame the integration of the two letters into one.

Subsequent commentators have not adopted Richard's thesis and the overall integrity of the letter is upheld except for one short section, that of 1 Thess. 2.13-16 (although sometimes verse 13 is considered authentic):

> We also constantly give thanks to God for this, that when you received the word of God that you heard from us, you accepted it not as a human word but as what it really is, God's word, which is also at work in you believers. For you, brothers and sisters, became imitators of the churches of God in Christ Jesus that are in Judea, for you suffered the same things from your own compatriots as they did from the Jews, who killed both the Lord Jesus and the prophets, and drove us out; they displease God and oppose everyone by hindering us from speaking to the Gentiles so that they may be saved. Thus they have constantly been filling up the measure of their sins; but God's wrath has overtaken them at last.

A number of reasons are put forth that challenge the authenticity of this text and suggest it is a later interpolation into 1 Thessalonians (see Pearson 1971). From a form-critical point of view, it is highly unusual for an ancient letter to include two separate thanksgiving sections, yet this text begins with a typical formula for a thanksgiving: 'we constantly give thanks to God' (2.13), whereas earlier in the letter we find the very similar formulation 'we always give thanks to God' (1.2). From a structural point of view, nothing is lost with the removal of 2.13-16, since 2.12 and 2.17 fit together well with no disruption of the argument. Yet these features alone are not sufficient to discount 2.13-16 as an interpolation.

More troubling is the content of these verses, both theologically and historically. The writers are harsh in their criticism of the Jews, noting not only Jewish culpability in the death of Jesus but also indicating that they are responsible for persecuting Christ believers in Judea and of driving Paul and his companions out of that province. Although they do not suggest it is Jews that are persecuting the believers at Thessalonike, they suggest the Gentile persecutors there are similar in their actions to Jews in Judea. This harsh anti-Jewish rhetoric runs counter, however, to Paul's theological reflections on Jews and Judaism in other letters, where he rarely refers to those involved in Jesus' death, despite often invoking the actual event.

Furthermore, when Paul does discuss Jews and Judaism he nuances his words carefully, with suggestions that while the Jewish requirement for male circumcision and dietary restrictions are no longer necessary 'in Christ', the Torah plays an important, instructive role in the life of God's chosen people (Galatians 3; Romans 7). More strikingly, when Paul reflects on the fate of the Jews in Romans 9–11 he seems to conclude that even those Jews who do not believe in Jesus will experience God's salvation. He is unsure how this will take place—he calls it a 'mystery'—but he knows it to be so, since God made such a promise to Abraham. Paul surmises that if God were not to save the non-believing Jews, God would be proved a liar. And if God lied to the Jews, who is to say that God is not lying about Christ? Paul concludes, 'a hardening has come upon part of Israel, until the full number of the Gentiles has come in. And so all Israel will be saved' (Rom. 11.25-26). This is very different from the seemingly full condemnation of Jews in 1 Thess. 2.15-16, where God's wrath 'has overtaken them at last'.

It is the past tense of this latter phrase that raises the historical issue with this text. While one might think of this wrath of God being God rejecting God's chosen people in the theological sense, the tone seems to indicate something much more concrete. Given that the writer is indicating something involving Jews living in Judea, one must look there for the reference. There is no doubt that life in Judea under Roman occupation was harsh for the Jews, and there are many instances of Roman insensitivity to the local populace and outright brutality against the people. Yet the one 'stand-out' historical event that radically altered Jewish self-understanding was their violent uprising against the Romans in 66 CE, which inaugurated a four-year struggle for independence. It did not end well, however, and in 70 CE the Roman general Titus breached the walls of Jerusalem and utterly destroyed the Temple—the focal point of Jewish religious life and the central place where Jews sacrificed to their God. This pivotal event marks the end of the sacrificial system, paving the way for the rise of rabbinic Judaism in the next century, and the Temple has never been rebuilt. Christ followers in the late first century and beyond believed this event was God's signal—a very powerful signal—that the Jewish religious system had come to an end. It was, to use their thinking, God's wrath coming upon God's formerly chosen people as a result of their rejection of Jesus (*Epistle of Barnabas* 16.3-4). This sounds very much like the language of 1 Thess. 2.15-16 and the overtaking of the Jews by God's wrath. Yet this event took place about a decade after Paul's death, and probably at least twenty years after the writing of 1 Thessalonians. Thus, many scholars posit that a later Christian writer added this little section to the original letter in order to highlight the consequences of rejecting Christ.

There is far from full agreement on 1 Thess. 2.13-16 being an interpolated passage. A number of scholars maintain that the controversial passage is in fact part of the original composition based on contextual and theological arguments. And one must note right up front that there is no textual evidence for its exclusion; that is, no ancient manuscripts are missing this particular section of text. Certainly the notion of the Thessalonians experiencing opposition and suffering noted in the passage fits with indications of suffering elsewhere in the letter: 'in spite of persecution you received the word with joy' (1.6); 'we had courage in our God to declare to you the gospel of God in spite of great opposition' (2.2). Likewise, the writers' reference to 'imitation' here echoes 1.6 (see further Weatherly 1991). Yet such similarities in language cut both ways, and one could argue that a later writer simply used words from the extant letter in composing the interpolation.

As a result, many scholars who argue for the authenticity of the text focus on explaining why the writers place the Jews in such a negative light here and how this fits with Pauline writings on this topic elsewhere. Thus, while they recognize the rather anti-Jewish sentiments in the text, they see these as mitigated by other circumstances. For example, Gilliard (1989) suggests that the focus on the blame in the text rests not on all Jews but only on those who were directly involved in putting Jesus to death; there is no universal condemnation of Jews intended here. Holtz (1990) extends this to include all Jews who act in opposition to God, sometimes expressed in their opposing Paul, but sees the text as still leaving the door open for Jews in general to obtain God's mercy. Donfried (1984) does see the condemnation of Jews construed more broadly, but interprets it as time-limited—God's wrath against the Jews lasts from the death of Jesus until the last day, when God's mercy is revealed. Other scholars take it in a different direction, acknowledging that the text is anti-Jewish, but no more so than what can be found in other texts written by Jewish writers (Lamp 2003). Schlueter (1994) sees in the text 'polemical hyperbole' that is similar to the tone Paul uses against Christians who oppose his work in other letters such as 2 Corinthians 11 and Galatians 2–5. They are condemned not because they are Jewish but because they oppose Paul's work.

When one looks at the various theories used to explain the anti-Jewish sentiments in this passage there is little emerging consistency of interpretation and it remains troublesome, not simply for its seeming promotion of anti-Judaism but its contradiction with other Pauline texts. Indeed, except for this latter issue, all of the explanations—interpolation, limited target, hyperbole—could seem to be special pleading on behalf of modern Christian interpreters who are uncomfortable with the legacy of Christian anti-Judaism and, later, anti-Semitism and its horrific outworking at the expense of many Jewish lives throughout history. Yet the contradictory nature of the text belies so simple an explanation and thus we must either attribute it to a later (anti-Jewish) Christian interpolation that reflects on the destruction of the Temple, or find an alternative explanation as to how it fits with Paul's writings elsewhere. I am particularly persuaded by the historical argument that the reference is to the Temple's destruction and post-dates Paul's death, thus it is an interpolation, but this is by no means a firm conviction and I'm sure the debate over this controversial text will continue.

Hearing the Letter

As we have seen, looking at the particular literary form of the written letter has proved to be an interesting way to delve into the social and theological content of the writing. Scholars also use another method to examine the written form of the text, a method they call 'rhetorical criticism'. Aristotle defines rhetoric as 'the means of persuasion in reference to any subject matter' (*Rhetoric* 1.2.1, LCL); it is an 'art', a learned skill that enables a person to convince other people about a point of view. Many scholars in the past three decades or so have analyzed Pauline letters to show how they employ ancient rhetorical strategies both in their overall structure and in the individual parts, revealing the writer's argumentative strategies. An analysis of the rhetoric also provides an indication of the social location of the recipients. A number of rhetorical strategies presuppose a certain social location and typical roles and functions of the audience.

Paul himself was not likely a technical rhetorician but he shared an educated person's familiarity with rhetoric, and one or more of his scribes might well have received formal training in rhetoric. And while ancient rhetoric was primarily focused on oral delivery, its application to written letters is justified by the fact that in antiquity, people did not read silently, not even when alone. Certainly when a Christ group received a letter from their founders they would gather to hear the letter read aloud, often by the person dispatched to deliver it. As we noted earlier, the letter becomes an aural rhetorical performance. Indeed, we know this oral reading to be the case, or at least the desire of the writers, since the final directive in 1 Thessalonians is very clear: 'I solemnly charge you in the Lord that this letter be read to all of the brothers' (5.27, my translation).

Three types of rhetorical speeches were distinguished in the ancient world: judicial, deliberative and epideictic (Aristotle, *Rhetoric* 1.3). Each has a specific function for a specific occasion. The goal of any rhetorical argument is to get the audience to act or think in a particular way. The occasion of a judicial speech is a trial before a judge or jury, whether in fact or as an assumed audience. The issue is the fact or legality of a certain action or actions that took place in the past. The means of persuasion is argument through accusation and defence and the categories being decided are whether the accused was 'just' or 'unjust'. The deliberative speech sees as its occasion a political debate within a council or assembly. The perceived audience of the speaker is comprised of 'critics' who have to be convinced, through persuasion and discussion, of the expediency or disadvantage of some future action. The issue is whether it will be more profitable to pursue one action over another. An epideictic speech takes place in the context of public occasions of memorial. Listeners are to be convinced concerning questions of honour and the grounds for praise or blame in the present time. Concepts of noble and disgraceful actions are contrasted. In epideictic rhetoric the dominant means of persuasion is encomium, or warmly enthusiastic praise.

When commentators apply these rhetorical labels to 1 Thessalonians, they arrive at divergent conclusions concerning the species of the rhetoric and its formal divisions, usually falling into one of two camps. Those who understand the letter as an example of deliberative rhetoric focus on Paul's attempts to persuade the Thessalonians to 'stand fast in the Lord' (3.8) or to adopt a particular lifestyle (4.1-8; 5.12-22) or belief (4.13-18; 5.1-11). Many others, however, have noticed that 1 Thessalonians is 'filled with praise for the readers because of their exemplary behavior', such as 1.2-3, 6-10; [2.13-14]; 2.19-20; 3.6-9; 4.1-2, 9-10 (Wanamaker 1990: 47). Even in the most obvious exhortation in the letter, 4.1-8, the writers are careful to reaffirm that the Thessalonians are already carrying out what is advocated, the writers are simply encouraging them to do so 'more and more' (4.1b; cf. 4.10). This emphasis on praise for that which is already being done in the present is characteristic of epideictic rhetoric. Thus, 1 Thessalonians is thought to be an example of epideictic rhetoric. Epideictic rhetoric sometimes includes a focus on action, particularly ethical actions. Commentators point to the urging of ethical action, sometimes referred to by the Greek word *paraenesis*, as further evidence that 1 Thessalonians fits into the rhetorical designation of epideictic (Wanamaker 1990: 48).

One possible way of sectioning the letter according to the ancient rhetorical divisions is the following:

1.1	The *prescript* in which the writers introduce themselves and identify their audience.
1.2–2.12	The *exordium* (including 2.13-16 if it is authentic) briefly introduces some topics that will be treated at length in the letter such as the strength of the Thessalonians' faith and their relationships with one another (1.3) as well as the coming of Christ (1.10). It also serves to establish the *ethos* of the writers by reminding the audience of the Paul party's prior interactions with the Thessalonians, which were largely positive, and their continuing concern to maintain this positive relationship.

2.17–3.13   The *narratio* reviews the Paul party's very positive past, present and future history together, noting their desire to be reunited and their affirmation that the Thessalonians continue in the way they are living out their commitment to the God of Jesus.

4.1–5.11   The *probatio* offers proof that the Thessalonians are the writers' 'glory and joy', while also addressing directly four issues or questions raised by the Thessalonians: proper sexual conduct (4.1-8), the nature of 'brotherly love' (4.9-12), the events around Jesus' coming appearance (4.13-18) and its timing (5.1-11). Throughout this section, the writers affirm the Thessalonians in what they are already doing (4.1, 10; 5.11).

5.12-22   In the *peroratio* the writers follow the rhetorical convention of including some ethical exhortations, in this case the urging of respect for community leaders and mutual concern for one another.

5.23-28   The *postscript* deviates from rhetorical strategies by returning to the letter format to include a number of elements typical of ancient letter closings more generally.

Using these divisions, the central concern of the letter, which occurs in the *narratio*, can be identified in 2.19-20: 'For what is our hope or joy or crown of boasting before our Lord Jesus at his coming? Is it not you? Yes, you are our glory and joy!' The writers reassure the Thessalonian believers that their faith is solid and they continue to care deeply for them.

Not all commentators divide the letter in precisely this way, as the chart below shows:

	Prescriptio	*Exordium*	*Narratio*	*Partitio*	*Probatio*	*Peroratio*	*Exhortatio*	*Closing*
Donfried 1993	-	1.1-10	2.1–3.10	3.11-13	4.1–5.3	5.4-11	-	5.12-22
Hughes 1990	-	1.1-10	2.1–3.10	3.11-13	4.1–5.3	5.4-11	5.12-22	5.23-28
Jewett 1986	-	1.1-5	1.6–3.13	-	4.1–5.22	5.23-28	-	-
Wanamaker 1990	1.1	1.2-10	2.1–3.10	3.11-13	4.1–5.22	5.23-28	-	-
Witherington 2006	1.1	1.2-3	1.4–3.10	3.11-13	4.1–5.15	5.16-22	-	5.23-28

The primary differences among them lies in their understanding of the extent of the *exordium* (the thanksgiving section) and the *probatio* ('proof' or evidence within the argument). Most commentators agree that the *probatio* includes 4.1–5.11, although some see it ending earlier in 1 Thessalonians 5 while others extend it to 5.22 or even to the end of the chapter at 5.28.

Concerns with the species, or type, of rhetoric in the letter as a whole was of particular concern to commentators in the late 1980s and throughout the 1990s. Walton (1995: 233-36) and Wanamaker (1990: 46-48) summarize the arguments used in some of these earlier attempts at classifying the letter. Hoppe (1997) surveys the different rhetorical breakdowns of 1 Thessalonians by earlier writers and found many conflicting opinions. To date, there has not been any emerging consensus on the rhetorical species of the letter as a whole or of the precise location of each rhetorical division. Each new commentator tends to offer a generic designation that best fits with her or his understanding of the overall purpose of the letter. Yet some attempts at identifying the rhetoric of a letter can seem circular: a letter is identified as 'judicial' because the content speaks to legal concerns, then the content is illuminated as legal *since* the letter is judicial. This is not, of course, always the case, and establishing the overall rhetorical genre of a letter can be helpful, although sometime more for identifying whether the writers deviate from the standard format than where they simply replicate it. After more than thirty years of work on the rhetorical species of 1 Thessalonians, it seems that the conclusion Hoppe reached over a decade ago (1997) still stands: while rhetorical analysis can lead to interesting exegetical insights, it alone cannot bring to light a full interpretation of the text (a sentiment supported by Wanamaker 2000).

The lack of consensus perhaps points to a deeper methodological question—namely, is it even appropriate to apply the strict categories of ancient rhetoric to letters? Some commentators think not, pointing out that rhetoric was intended for written speeches performed before an audience, while letters were less concerned with the performative aspects of communication (so Malherbe 1992: 279-93). Thus, letters, including Paul's letters, should not be classified as a whole according to one particular genre of rhetoric. This position does not deny, however, that individual sections of a letter might follow the structure of a particular type of rhetorical argument—deliberative, judicial, epideictic—but letters as a whole belie such structure. Thus, many commentators simply do not offer any suggested divisions according to rhetorical categories (e.g. Fee 2009), or reject them outright as unhelpful (e.g. Malherbe 2000: 96; Green 2002: 72; Beale 2003: 24).

Vernon Robbins (2009) and scholars working on the Rhetoric of Religious Antiquity project are advocating a new way forward in socio-rhetorical analysis (disclosure: I am one such scholar!). As with many other scholars, Robbins rightly rejects the outmoded notion that letters are simply replacements for rhetorical speeches. While letters are read aloud, they have their own characteristics, informed by modes of oral performance and modes of written performance. Rather than simply identifying the parts of Pauline letters according to the categories of ancient rhetorical handbooks, Robbins and his colleagues are attempting to interpret texts as representing a slice of social, cultural and ideological communication insofar as each piece evokes a constellation of networks of meaning. There are two aspects to every text: the mental images that are evoked and the argumentative strategies that are employed. While traditional rhetorical criticism focuses somewhat on this latter aspect, Robbins suggests that what is missing is consideration of how word-pictures work with the thought-statements to produce new meanings within a given context for the audience. Examination of the textual blending of images and arguments can produce, Robbins maintains, new interpretive insights into the texts of the New Testament. Initial ventures into this area suggest he is correct.

Having now examined how the writers constructed their letter to the Thessalonians, we can turn our attention to how two key themes that run through the letter are played out in the various sections. The first theme is the affirmation of the relationship between the Paul party and the Christ group in the city (Chapter 3). The second is the advice the writers give the Thessalonians on how to remain faithful in the face of moral challenges and their impending mortality (Chapter 4). The writers' use of rhetorical strategies can be set alongside broader cultural references from their time in order to allow us—the modern readers—to grasp the impact that the writers were attempting to have by sending the letter to the Thessalonian Christ group.

AFFIRMING RELATIONSHIPS

In the mind of Paul and his co-writers, the relationship they have with the Thessalonians is very positive—it began that way and continued after they left the city, at least that's what they thought. When Timothy returns to Paul and Silvanus in Corinth, he seems to bring word that the Thessalonian Christ believers are grumbling over what seemed to them to be an abrupt and unexplained departure by the Paul party. We do not know the exact nature of their complaints. As is so often the case, all we can do is mirror-read the letters to determine the nature of the problems that are being addressed. Doing so with 1 Thess. 2.1-20 suggests that Paul and his companions are very much concerned with defending their decision to leave while reassuring the Thessalonians of their deep and abiding interest in their wellbeing. In the first section of this chapter, we will look in some detail at how the letter writers present their case. In section two we will look at another aspect of the Thessalonian Christ believers' ongoing relationship with the Paul party by examining the letter's thanksgiving section (1.2-10), in which the writers recount for the Thessalonians how wonderful it has been to find that they have been proclaiming the Paul party's honours and boasting about their allegiance to a new deity. Finally, we will jump to the end of the letter to look briefly at the writers' urging of respect for what seems to be a local leadership team (5.12-22). Together these three sections of the letter reflect the next stage of the story of the Christ group at Thessalonike: despite their disappointment over the quick departure of the Paul party, they continued to honour them, and now, they are told, should do likewise with the leaders who are currently taking care of their group.

Oh Brother, Where Art Thou? (2.1-20)

In the ancient world, much like today, any number of people were willing to set aside their moral compass and exploit others in order to take away their money. To do so, they gain the victim's confidence and, somewhat innocuously, ask for a 'loan' or some such thing. With money in hand, they disappear, never to be heard of again. Such people populate the literature of the Greco-Roman world. One example is Peregrinus, found in the writings of a second-century satirist named Lucian. According to Lucian, Peregrinus' one great desire in life was to become a famous philosopher and be honoured in every town he visited. He pretended that he could hear the voice of a snake telling him the future in order to convince people that he had a direct line to the gods. In the end, such was his quest for notoriety and his desire to be remembered long past his death that he threw himself onto a burning pyre in Olympia and died before the eyes of the townsfolk (Lucian, *The Passing of Peregrinus*, 1). In some respects, he got what he wanted—to be remembered, but perhaps not the way he had hoped, since Lucian memorializes him in print as a charlatan and a fool.

In the second chapter of 1 Thessalonians the writers seem to be on the defensive about their actions while they lived and worked among the Thessalonians. Some scholars have suggested that this defensive tone reflects a situation where Paul and his co-workers made a hasty departure from the city and have yet to return. Perhaps there was grumbling against them, accusing them of spinning a story about an all-powerful God who would bring about vengeance and reward in the near future simply as a means of separating the Thessalonians from their money. The writers assert that this is not the case. The opening section (2.1-12) outlines all of this, and seems to be responding point by point to a number of accusations. Taken together, the accusations behind these defensive statements would add up to one thing—that the members of the Paul party were charlatans, no better than the likes of Peregrinus.

It is difficult to determine with any amount of certainty whether Paul and his companions were actually accused by some of the Thessalonians of being false preachers or whether they just anticipate being so accused or even are simply using self-defence as a rhetorical strategy (Malherbe 1970; Walton 1995). Whether the accusations are real or imagined, however, the writers have structured their argument so that any Christ follower at Thessalonike who might question the Paul party's integrity ends up actually raising a question about their own community's integrity. In the opening thanksgiving section the writers note that the Thessalonians 'became imitators of us and of the Lord' (1.6, cf. 4.1). If Paul and his companions acted disgracefully, then as 'imitators' so do the Thessalonian Christ followers. It is a clever rhetorical move, but in 1 Thessalonians 2 the writers employ a much more substantive defence.

The writers' defensive strategy takes the form of self-recommendation. They note that when they came to Thessalonike they had the full approval of God (2.4). Clearly, the letter writers are very much concerned to maintain a positive relationship with the Thessalonians, one that goes well beyond that of speaker-listener: 'so deeply do we care for you that we are determined to share with you not only the gospel of God but also our own selves, because you have become very dear to us' (2.8). In order to demonstrate their commitment to maintaining this relationship, the writers offer evidence of their integrity. They open the whole section by narrating how they behaved among the Thessalonians.

The writers note that when they first arrived from Philippi, where they had undergone considerable opposition, they set about to proclaim the message despite experiencing conflict once again: 'we had courage…to declare to you the gospel of God' (2.2). The expression that the writers use here is a technical term that arises from the Greco-Roman philosophical tradition of 'frankness' or 'bold speech' (*parrēsia*). Greek philosophers drew attention to freedom of speech and the courage to speak in the face of opposition. In political contexts, it meant resisting civic authorities when they tried to subdue the voice of the populace who were protesting for justice. Such expressions were particularly characteristic of ancient philosophers such as the Stoics and, to a greater degree, the Cynics.

This latter group gets its name from a derogatory nickname that was given to them—'dogs'. While meant as an insult because they were wild and dirty like the street mongrels of antiquity, always nipping at passersby or disturbing people with their loud barking, the Cynics' founder, Diogenes, actually liked the nickname. The story goes that once when he was at a banquet, some of the diners kept throwing the bones to him as if he were a dog. In response, Diogenes 'played a dog's trick' and urinated on them (Diogenes Laertius, 'Diogenes', *Lives of Eminent Philosophers* VI.2.46). By invoking the tradition of 'bold speech', the writers of 1 Thessalonians are indicating that like the Stoics or Cynics they are not afraid to 'tell it like it is' or undertake risky behaviour. Although it might be easier to avoid conflict, the Paul party boldly proclaimed the unpopular message of the superiority of their God to those with whom they were working.

In the ensuing defence of their actions the writers place a heavy emphasis on their personal integrity, opening with a list of what is not characteristic of their 'appeal': error, uncleanness, deceit (2.3). In contrast, they assert that they have been 'tested' or 'approved' by God (2.4), an image that has resonance in both the Jewish scriptures and Greco-Roman political contexts of the time. In the Hebrew Bible, God often tests God's chosen people, both collectively and individually. For example, it is through the testing of their hearts that God determines whether the people of Israel have strayed from the covenant relationship, or when a prophet such as Jeremiah is called to duty as God's spokesperson, his heart is first tested. In the Greco-Roman world, the suitability of a citizen who desired to take up political office was tested by examination of his character. Any flaws such as deceitfulness, crookedness and selfish ambition would be cause for his removal from the ballot, or from office if he happened to get there.

The writers continue with the litany of what does not characterize their time among the Thessalonians: they were not flatterers, nor greedy, nor seeking honour, despite the fact that as leaders they might have claimed honour (2.5-7a). These are precisely the kinds of things that one would expect in false philosophers such as Peregrinus. They would use their clever words to construct arguments to make their audience well disposed towards them, all with the intent of receiving much by way of cash donations for them to continue their work. This is just the kind of thing Paul and his companions claim to have avoided.

Finally, having given an account of what they did not do, in contrast to the false preachers of the time, the writers provide the Thessalonians with a positive image of their behaviour: 'But we were gentle among you, like a nurse tenderly caring for her own children' (2.7b). The word 'nurse' is more akin to what we might call a 'nanny'. It is not referencing a medical practitioner; it is a domestic image, one that evokes concern and nurturing. Elite households often employed one or more nannies to bring up children. The nanny would make major decisions for a child in her care, ranging from choices of food and clothing to where and how a child would be educated. Many of the extant Greek and Roman philosophical and literary works were written by elites, who sometimes expressed their fond recollections of the lasting influence their nanny had on them. And when used as a metaphor, it signalled the deep and abiding relationship between a philosopher and his students.

Thus, by using the 'nanny' image here, the writers again draw on imagery from the philosophical tradition. The image of a nurse was used to show how a true philosopher would vary his style of speech according to the needs of the audience. When in need of rebuke, he would use harsh scolding, but when the audience would profit most from encouragement, the philosopher would become gentle and comforting. In the case of the Thessalonians, however, the writers intensify the image by noting that their actions were not that of a nanny with someone else's children, but that of a nanny caring for her own daughters and sons. The argument is one of 'from the lesser to the greater': if a nanny cares deeply for the children of another mother, *how much more* would she care for her very own children. The writers assure the Thessalonians that they shared their very souls (*psychē*) with them (2.8). This sentiment expresses deep affection and yearning, not unlike depictions of parents' sad yearning for a deceased child one might find on ancient grave inscriptions.

The material in 2.1-8 is a rather lengthy initial proof of the Paul party's integrity, which is followed by three much shorter, argumentative demonstrations. The first of these is an accounting of their self-sufficiency. We noted earlier the conditions under which the Paul party spread the message—the workshop. Now they mention this as part of the larger self-justification strategy. Unlike many wandering philosophers (both good and bad), while in Thessalonike the Paul party did not rely on patrons for food and lodging nor did they charge listeners for their messages. The writers are adamant that they did not evidence greed (2.5) and did not demand or receive any payment from the Thessalonians, despite the fact that they had very right to do so (2.6). Instead they supported themselves by working 'night and day' in order not to be a burden to them (2.9). The reference to their 'labour' and 'toil' stress the exhaustion that they underwent just to avoid being burdensome to others.

The writers also point to the quality of their conduct among the Thessalonians that comprised the Christ group. In 2.10, the writers draw attention to their typical way of behaving: 'you are witnesses, and God also, how pure, upright, and blameless our conduct was toward you believers'. This is not just about their character. Rather, they draw specific attention to the quality of their behavior, which may also be rendered 'godliness' and 'justice'. Against any thought or charges of deviance being brought against them, the writers note that the quality of their action among the Thessalonians manifests their underlying integrity of character.

In the very next verse they turn their attention to the quality of instruction they delivered to the Thessalonians: 'we dealt with each one of you like a father with his children' (2.11). The writers use the metaphor of fatherhood, drawing upon the Roman (and Greek) notion that the oldest living male in a family, the *paterfamilias*, is responsible for each and every person living under his roof, including extended family members, friends, workers and even slaves. The *paterfamilias* was responsible for each family member's moral instruction, especially that of the children. The writers remind the Thessalonians that the instruction they provided advocated for them literally to 'walk worthy of God' (2.12), just the kind of instruction an honourable *paterfamilias* would be expected to provide.

Recognizing that it may not be enough simply to remind the Thessalonian Christ group of the characteristics of their past interactions, the writers next turn their attention to the present and future relationship, building on their earlier claim that they so deeply cared for them that they were ready to put their lives in the hands of the Thessalonians (2.8). In the section that runs from 2.17 through 3.10 the writers address head-on their physical absence from Thessalonike, noting that they were not absent 'in heart', and 'longed with great eagerness' to see them in person (2.17), but their best efforts to do so were blocked by Satan (2.18), although the letter is rather vague on the details of how or where this happened. Paul himself interjects his own special message into the broader desire of the entire Paul party by noting that he desired to return 'again and again' (2.18). As we noted in Chapter 2, a committee wrote the letter, but this little insertion by Paul indicates that he is the perceived leader, both among the writers themselves and by the Christ followers at Thessalonike. This desire to see the Thessalonians seems very much reciprocated, according to the report Timothy brought back from his visit to the city (3.6).

In order to reassure them further, they write, 'For what is our hope or joy or crown of boasting before our Lord Jesus at his coming? Is it not you? Yes, you are our glory and joy!' (2.19-20). There is a shift in chronology here, from the present to the future, and a reminder to the Thessalonians that it was this concern for the future that made an impression on them in the first place (cf. 1.9-10). Crowning was an important aspect of honourifics in antiquity. In associations, crowns were often used as a means to bestow glory on a founder or patron of the group. In the following example, one individual named Dionysodoros is honoured by four different associations for his patronage of each. Dionysodoros was so pleased with the honours bestowed upon him by these associations that he had their proclamations re-inscribed on a single monument. We will quote below the section recorded by the first of these associations, with its extensive use of crowning:

> The head of the club of the Haliasts and Haliads, Dionysodoros the Alexandrian, benefactor, having been praised and crowned for virtue with a gold crown by the association of Dionysiasts and having been honored for his benefaction and with freedom from service of all kinds; and, having been crowned with two gold crowns in the reception of the Baccheia during the triennial festival by his fellow club members, who have received benefactions from him, he made a dedication to triennial festival personified and to the association (*AGRW* 255, Rhodes, second century BCE).

The other three sections follow a similar format and likewise make multiple references to crowns.

Unlike Dionysodoros, who was keen to have his honours publicized, the writers of 1 Thessalonians note that they did not seek such honours while they were among the Thessalonians (2.6a). In 2.19-20 they say that they received it anyway, but not in the tangible, costly manner of a laurel wreath or golden crown. Collectively, the Thessalonian association is the mark of honour that the Paul party bears; the Thessalonians are their crown at the coming of Jesus. This is the central theme of the entire letter. The latter part of the letter (1 Thessalonians 4–5) affirms them in their behaviour, encouraging them to continuing living out the lessons they learned 'more and more' (4.1). As we shall see, the thanksgiving section of the letter's opening chapter emphasizes the positive, public relationship between the Thessalonian Christ group and the Paul party upon which this whole argument in 1 Thessalonians 2 builds.

Mission? Impossible! (1.2-10)

As we discussed in Chapter 2, the form of the ancient letter included an early section in which some sort of health wish or thanksgiving was expressed. In 1 Thessalonians this occurs in 1.2-10. And as is the case with ancient letters, the thanksgiving section is not simply a matter of well-wishing. Rather, it provides an introduction to some of the main themes of the letter and is an opportunity for writers to establish a foundation for the next sections. In the case of 1 Thessalonians, the thanksgiving section provides the writers with the opportunity to remind the Thessalonians about their extant relationship as it was established through their having brought the gospel message to Thessalonike and, more importantly, the Thessalonians' reception of it. Even more, the writers emphasize the enduring results of the 'gospel' (*euangelion*) in grounding 'your work of faith and labor of love and steadfastness of hope in our Lord Jesus Christ' (1.3). This is the first of two instances in this letter in which the triad of faith, hope and love is used (cf. 5.8). In this case, each word is preceded by a reference that anticipates the writers' concern to emphasize the working class status they share with the recipients: 'work', 'labour' and 'endurance'.

While this triad reflects the results of their having been receptive to the message of the Paul party, the remaining verses recount the manner in which they received that message, and what happened as a result. The writers note that the gospel came to the Thessalonians 'in power and in the Holy Spirit', evidence that God had chosen them to be open and receptive to it (1.4-5). Indeed, the writers underline that the Thessalonians 'know what kind of persons we proved to be among you for your sake' (1.5), likely anticipating their self-justification in the next section (2.1-20), as we discussed above. Upon hearing the message, likely over many days and weeks, the Thessalonians came to accept it, despite the hardship it entailed, and as a result began to act much like the members of the Paul party: 'you became imitators of us and of the Lord, for in spite of persecution you received the word with joy inspired by the Holy Spirit' (1.6). This is the only place in the Pauline letters where the audience is acknowledged to be already imitating Paul and his companions rather than being exhorted to do so (see 1 Cor. 4.16; 11.1; Phil. 3.17; cf. 2 Thess. 3.7-9; Eph. 5.1). As a result of this imitation, the Thessalonians became an example for people throughout the area: 'For the word of the Lord has sounded forth from you not only in Macedonia and Achaia, but in every place your faith in God has become known, so that we have no need to speak about it' (1.8).

The writers are pleased that news has been spreading from Thessalonike throughout the Roman provinces of Macedonia and Achaia (Greece). For modern interpreters, however, there is some question as to how this news was spread. Most commentators on this text understand it to indicate that the Thessalonians have undertaken some form of what we may call 'missionary' activity. This is the nature of their 'imitation' of the Paul party; they too are now going into public places in order to proclaim the gospel and facilitate others giving their full allegiance to God through Christ (Frame 1912: 76; Bruce 1982: 15-16; Malherbe 2000: 117). James Ware (1992) is particularly persuasive in this regard, referring to the Thessalonians as a 'missionary congregation', although without giving too much detail as to how they went about proclaiming the message.

It is this latter issue of 'how' that has caused a few others to question whether the notion of 'missionaries' is adequate to describe how the Thessalonians are imitating Paul. Dickson (2003: 97-103) has looked at the Greek text in detail to suggest that the grammar does not really support the conclusions drawn by Ware and others that follow him. Rather than suggest that the Thessalonians are actively preaching the gospel, the text focuses on the news *about* the Thessalonians and their change of allegiance (see also Bowers 1991; Reinmuth 1998: 121; Coulot 2006). That is to say, while not ignoring the reason for their behaviour (the gospel message), the focus of the news is the fact *that* they undertook the radical step of changing their allegiance from an assortment of protective deities to put all their stock in a single God. In order to demonstrate how this might have happened, we can turn again to typical behaviours of associations, and pick up our earlier narrative of the Paul party in Thessalonike (the following picture is a summary of Ascough 2014, which provides the technical justifications for it).

Paul and his companions settled into the workshop and chatted among the other workers there, eventually convincing them to change their allegiance to the God of Jesus. Soon afterwards, they departed from the city, heading east along the *Via Egnatia* to Beroea, after which they turned south, eventually arriving in the Roman province of Achaia, where they stayed in Athens. After some time there, they moved to Corinth, which is the likely place where Timothy returns to them after his visit to and from Thessalonike. As they made their way along the eastern and southern roads they would continue their recruitment efforts. Yet unlike in other places, here the news is not really news because the people have already heard about their impact in Thessalonike. It seems to the Paul party that 'in every place your faith in God has become known, so that we have no need to speak about it' (1.8).

As we noted, the usual explanation is that the Thessalonians have dispatched missionaries that have preceded the Paul party along the eastern and southern roads. Yet this is problematic on a few fronts. First, while one can often admire the zeal of the newly converted, that the non-Jewish hand workers of Thessalonike would be able to be dispatched so soon after their radical change of allegiance to God and effectively proclaim the complex theological message of the gospel seems rather far-fetched. Paul, we know, was quite well educated in Judaism, having trained as a Pharisee, and as such would be adept at public speaking and rhetorical argumentation. The majority of artisans, on the other hand, began their apprenticeships early in life, perhaps around six or seven years old, and thus were not trained rhetoricians. Thus, this is not likely the nature of the Thessalonians' 'imitation'. Second, as we noted in the previous section, the Paul party seemed to have made a hasty departure from Thessalonike, suggesting they did not stay there particularly long. We might ask, then, how the Thessalonian mission-aries managed to have such an impact given the short time frame for their work.

Critical to this discussion, and too often overlooked, is the letter writers' description of the nature of the news that has spread, for it is news about the Thessalonians rather than news about God: their *faith* has become known (1.8), including their turning to God from idols (1.9). More striking, the writers note that 'the people of those regions report about us what kind of welcome we had among you' (1.9). That is, the focus of the reports is on the reception of the Paul party by the Thessalonians. This is the news that is 'sounding forth' from the Thessalonike Christ group.

Associations at the time regularly proclaimed in public honours for their founders and patrons, eventually setting up inscriptions for them. The fol-lowing text from a second-century BCE inscription from the Piraeus is some-what typical of the type of language we find in honours proclaimed for founders. We quote below the first part of the association's resolution to honour a man for his deeds:

> Whereas it has happened that Dionysios has left this life, and he had dis-played in many things the goodwill that he had and continued to have toward all who brought the association together for the god. Also, when he was asked he was always the cause of some good thing, both for individu-als and for the common good, being a benefactor at all times. Whereas he has already been honored by the Dionysiasts, he has received the priest-hood of the god, and he has been appointed treasurer, further increasing the common revenues by contributing one thousand silver drachmas from his own resources. And after all of the other expenditures he contributed a place in which they could come and sacrifice each month to the god in accordance with their ancestral customs (*AGRW* 21, 176/175 BCE).

The inscription continues on for many more lines, outlining all of the finan-cial and administrative contributions Dionysios made to the association.

Such inscriptions were not likely set up by the Thessalonian Christ group, at least not in its early stages of development. But inscriptions were never the first method of proclamation in associations. Before being inscribed, such honours were announced at group meetings and sometimes even pro-claimed in the public square. In the case of the inscription just quoted, it clearly was resolved orally within the group, since the final lines record the requirement that it *also* be inscribed on behalf of the group: 'Let this decree be inscribed on a stone monument and erected beside the sanctuary of the god. The cost of the monument and its erection shall be borne by the treasurer.'

The other form of proclamation typical of associations involved honour-ing deities for their support and divine patronage of the group, often listing all the good things the god had accomplished. One of the ways this takes place is the narration of a foundational story. We quoted one such inscription in Chapter 1—the story of Sarapis being introduced into the Macedonian town of Opus (*AGRW* 52). Such stories not only honour the deity; they are expressions of collective devotion on the part of the group. They also serve to enhance the honour of the group in showing how they garnered divine favour.

Drawing on such typical behaviours among associations, we can suggest that once the Thessalonian workers' association had decided to change their allegiance from 'idols' to 'the living and true' God whose son Jesus would bring salvation from the heavens (1.9-10), they began to advertise that fact as a means to honour both God and the Paul party. The Thessalonian Christ group was acting locally in proclaiming their new allegiance to friends, neighbours, merchants and customers. Nevertheless, these proclamations became the source of news about the Thessalonians that travelled throughout the networks of the region. The *Via Egnatia* was a primary artery for trade and commerce in the Roman world, as was the shipping port at Thessalonike. There was a constant flow of goods in and out of the city, and, of course, seamen, dockworkers, small traders, artisans, shop owners and customers would handle these goods. At each transaction people would talk, and without access to things we often take for granted such as newspapers or the internet, the talk would focus on local news and gossip.

The members of the Thessalonian Christ group likely described to their friends, family and business associates how their change of allegiance occurred, perhaps boasting about how wise men from the eastern extent of the empire came to them with a warning about a 'coming wrath' and the means of escape (1.9-10). In telling the story, they would make it interesting, narrating their initial resistance and the persistence of this group of strangers among them, finally conveying how their change of allegiance took place. As their narrative took shape, they began to move it out into the public realm, advertising the benefits that had accrued to them as a result of their change of allegiance. Again, this was typical association behaviour. Such public polemics served not only as a form of recruitment (i.e. 'if you join our group, look what you get'), but also as a way of asserting their superiority over other groups. It was a way of saying, 'look how much better our group is than your group'. This would explain why the letter writers note 'trouble' or 'tribulation' the Thessalonians experienced (1.6, often misleadingly translated as 'persecution'); other groups would retaliate by asserting their own predominance.

There would have been quite a number of itinerant people among those who heard the stories of the workers group's allegiance change and the foreign agents who helped bring it about. These itinerants would include merchants who travelled frequently among the trade networks of the regions, and likely included a number of local Thessalonians who likewise travelled for work. In travelling from place to place they would have plenty of time to chat with one another and exchange lots of gossip. In each new city, they would share their news and gossip with their contacts there. We can imagine that behind the 'reports' the letter writers reference in 1.8 there was a wide variety of responses, ranging from recognizing the 'bravery' of a small workers' association that had placed its trust in a single foreign god, to incredulity that they would go down this path of 'atheism'.

The travellers sharing this news in other towns might have included some of the Thessalonian Christ followers, but there is no basis for assuming they were acting exclusively or even primarily as 'missionaries'. They are simply doing what travellers do—talking with their companions about things of importance while they go about their business. For Paul and his companions it could seem like 'everyone' was talking about what had taken place among the Thessalonian Christ group, but this simply reflects that fact that the Paul party was traversing the same path, and thus following in the wake of those who had travelled, and gossiped, along the routes before them.

Lead On! (5.12-22)

Although the foregoing two sections of this chapter have focused primarily on the relationship that existed between the Paul party and the Thessalonian Christ group, they also raise the issue of the nature of leadership within the group itself. During its formative stage the group relied on Paul and his companions to provide guidance on conduct and belief, and their suddenly going AWOL created a bit of a crisis. Nevertheless, the group continued to flourish, proclaiming honours upon these absent leaders, news of which spread to other cities. Yet the inability of the founders to return in due course would seem to create a leadership vacuum. Some keen persons would step up to take on the organization and maintenance of the group. If our initial suggestion that the group was formed by a reorientation of an already extant group is correct, then there would have been in place protocols for the electing or appointing of leaders.

Unlike in letters written to other locales, in 1 Thessalonians Paul and his companions do not name any of the local people. The only indication that we have from the writers that there are active leaders among the Thessalonian Christ group comes towards the end of the letter, when they write, 'we appeal to you, brothers and sisters, to respect those who labor among you, and have charge of you in the Lord and admonish you; esteem them very highly in love because of their work' (5.12-13a). The concluding statement is very important: 'be at peace among yourselves' (5.13b). Associations were well known for the disorderly behaviour they regularly exhibited at meetings, something we will explore in detail in Chapter 6.

By appending this imperative to the affirmation of local leadership, the writers recall their response to the Thessalonians' own question about how they are to live and work together, to which they were told 'quietly and lovingly' (4.9-11).

The list of 'dos' and a few 'don'ts' that the writers include follows the format of the types of ethical imperatives one might find in ancient philosophical literature. A number of these commendations and admonitions focus on communal behaviours, and as such are practical ways in which the members (the 'brothers and sisters' of 5.14) can give practical expression to loving and esteeming their leaders, namely, by aiding them in their tasks:

- admonish the disorderly,
- comfort the discouraged,
- stand with the weak,
- be patient towards all.

This is all summarized by a much more general admonition against retaliatory behaviours and the pursuit of the greatest good for everyone: 'see to it that no one should repay evil for evil, and always pursue the good for one another and for everyone' (5.15, my translation). Although briefly listed, and without much commentary, these admonitions would seem radically counter-cultural to the hearers of the letter. As part of a collectivist culture they thrived on competitiveness and the besting of others in all matters great and small. Anyone who broke the rules, lost hope, showed weakness or fell out of line in other ways could be exploited for selfish gain on an individual level. According to the letter writers, however, such persons are to be coaxed back into the group; this is part of the community commitment.

In the second set of imperatives there is a grammatical change insofar as the verbs are now placed after the adverbs, which is quite unusual in Greek. It demarcates that the writers are moving to a slightly different context, albeit one in keeping with the communal focus of the first set of imperatives. Although sometimes taken by modern readers as admonitions for personal piety, these actions are meant for the gathered community and thus give us a picture of what their worship might have looked like. All three imperatives are grounded in 'the will of God for you in Christ Jesus' (5.18):

- always rejoice,
- unceasingly pray,
- in everything give thanks.

To this list, the writers add one more set of admonitions, fleshing them out in more detail, probably because they are a source of concern within the community:

- the Spirit do not extinguish,
- prophecy do not despise,
- everything test,
- the good hold,
- from every form of evil abstain.

Although the last three imperatives (test, hold, abstain) have long been interpreted as an exhortation towards personal morality, in this text they are very much focused on the context of cult activity within the group and speak to communal behaviour in the face of some members speaking words as if from God ('prophecy'). These words are not to be discounted out of hand, but nor is every utterance to be taken at face value. The writers thus urge that such expressions of divine words be tested and those that are deemed to be of an 'evil' kind are to be discounted and those that are deemed 'good' are to be heeded (for the linguistic arguments for this interpretation, see Fee 2009: 222-24). Indeed, treating good prophecy as anything but good would be to 'quench the Spirit' (5.19).

In the brief text encompassed by 1 Thess. 5.12-22, the letter writers provide their support for the local leadership while placing responsibility on others within the group to support them by regulating one another's behaviours. There are, however, some more complex issues about which the Thessalonians seem to have asked the Paul party for guidance. We will turn our attention to these in the next chapter.

STANDING FIRM IN TROUBLING TIMES

Paul and his co-writers seem quite pleased overall with the Thessalonian Christ group, affirming and praising them for their 'faith, hope, and love', which is expressed outwardly through work, labour and endurance (1.3) and urged inwardly as a defensive strategy through military metaphors ('breast-plate' and 'helmet', 5.8). The bulk of the first part of the letter is spent reaffirming the relationship that the Paul party shares with the Thessalonians, culminating with the narrating of Timothy's return and the deep longing they share to return to Thessalonike:

> Timothy has just now come to us from you, and has brought us the good news of your faith and love. He has told us also that you always remember us kindly and long to see us—just as we long to see you (3.7).

It seems, however, that Timothy has also brought news of some questions and issues with which the Thessalonians are struggling and the letter writers turn their attention to addressing them head-on, in order to help the Christ adherents to 'continue to stand firm in the Lord' (3.8).

In 1 Thessalonians 4 and 5, four issues are addressed, each with a construction to suggest that it has been brought to the writers' attention by the Thessalonians themselves, either through Timothy's oral report or in a letter carried by him:

- 'Brothers and sisters…as you learned from us how you ought to live and to please God…you should do so more and more' (4.1);
- 'Now concerning love of the brothers and sisters' (4.9);
- 'But we do not want you to be uninformed, brothers and sisters' (4.13);
- 'Now concerning the times and the seasons' (5.1).

The first and second issues together address community interactions, the first focused on the need for maintaining sexual purity and the second on the need for practical expressions of mutual care and concern. The latter two issues are concerned with the end of days and are intimately connected despite addressing what were probably two separate questions: when will it happen, and will those who have already died miss out? We will treat these latter two issues together, after first looking at how the letter writers address the issues of sexual purity and mutual care.

Sexual Shenanigans (4.1-8)

The section following the letter writers' review and verification of their positive relationship with the Thessalonian believers begins with an affirmation of the Thessalonians' behaviour:

> Finally, brothers and sisters, we ask and urge you in the Lord Jesus that, as you learned from us how you ought to live and to please God (as, in fact, you are doing), you should do so more and more. For you know what instructions we gave you through the Lord Jesus (4.1-2).

They know the instructions, learned well how to live, and are already doing what is necessary, yet they need to do so 'more and more'. There are no new lessons to be learned. That said, however, one particular issue seems to need some bolstering. A number of references in this section indicate that the focus is sexual ethics: 'sexual immorality' (*porneia*, 4.3), 'lust' (*epithymia*, 4.5) and 'impurity' (*akatharsia*, 4.7). Nevertheless, precisely what is the problem is not very clear, in part due to the metaphor the writers use in 4.4 when asserting that it is God's will that 'each one of you know how to *ktasthai* your own *skeuos* in holiness and honor'. The Greek verb *ktasthai* indicates 'control' or 'acquire', two related but different actions. The word *skeuos* literally indicates a 'vessel', 'tool' or 'utensil', but its metaphoric value is a point of ongoing scholarly debate. How it is translated is the linchpin for understanding what is being advocated in this passage.

The NRSV translates this verse as 'each one of you know how to control your own body in holiness and honor', but this is only one possible translation. The Revised Standard Version translates it as 'each one of you know how to take a wife for himself in holiness and honour', which is a far cry from controlling your own body. Other renderings include:

- 'each of you should learn to control your own body in a way that is holy and honorable' (NIV);
- 'Respect and honor your wife' (CEV);
- 'each of you will control his own body and live in holiness and honor' (NLT);
- 'each of you should know how to live with your wife in a holy and honorable way' (GNT);
- 'learn to appreciate and give dignity to your body, not abusing it' (*The Message*).

Some translations leave the verse somewhat obscure with a version of 'each of you know how to possess his own vessel in sanctification and honour',

most of them including some footnotes to indicate the translational problems (e.g. NASB, KJV). This has not satisfied commentators, who have wres-
tled with the meaning of the word since at least the fourth century CE to the
present day (Wanamaker 1990: 152). A variety of solutions are proffered,
but they can be boiled down to three basic possibilities for rendering the
word *skeuos* into English: 'wife', 'body' and 'male genitalia'.

In some contexts, *skeuos* is used to refer to a man's 'wife' (Collins 1984:
313; Malherbe 2000: 227; Witherington 2006: 114-16), in part because, in
the eyes of the ancients, a male 'possessed' his wife and children in the legal
sense of the word. Thus, the letter writers could be advocating 'obtaining' a
wife through marriage in order to avoid sexual temptation outside of bonds of
marriage (Burke 2003: 187-96). On the other hand, they might be suggesting
that a man 'control' his wife in the sense of taking responsibility for his wife's
action and preventing her from acting outside societal norms. Bassler (1995)
goes a bit farther along this vector and suggests that the writers are advocating 'spiritual marriages' in which both partners remain chaste.

A second context in which the Greek word *skeuos* can be used is with
reference to a person's physical 'body'. If this is the sense in 1 Thessalonians then the writers' recommendation is addressing directly the need to
control desire (McGehee 1989; Morris 1991: 124; Richard 1995: 197-98),
particularly that of a sexual nature. It may even be a more general urging
towards purity in body and mind (Verhoef 1997). Using semantic evidence,
however, J. Smith (2001) concludes that the writers advocate general bodily
control, perhaps with the more specific reference to control of the male
sexual organ.

This brings us to the third option, and the one that I find most persuasive: *skeuos* is a reference to the male genitalia (see Wanamaker 1990: 152-
53; Ascough 2003: 187-89). In the second-century Greek translation of the
Hebrew Bible, called the Septuagint, the Greek word *skeuos* is used in a
context in which it clearly indicates the male sexual organ. In responding to
a question about whether the young men have kept themselves from women,
David assures the priest of Nob that 'the young men's *vessels* are holy' (1
Sam. 21.5; see Whitton 1982). In addition, a fragmentary second-century
BCE text found at Qumran, the location of the Dead Sea Scrolls, makes reference to 'the *vessel* of your bosom', which contextually is a euphemism for
the male sex organ (Elgvin 1997). It has similar uses in non-biblical Greek
writings as well (see Donfried 1985: 342). All of this to say, there are clear
antecedents for the metaphoric use of the word *skeuos* for 'male genitalia'.

Perhaps more importantly, however, is the overall thrust of the argument
in 1 Thess. 4.1-8, which is really focused on the impact that sexual ethics
has on community relationships. The passage ends with a rather harsh warning that no one is to wrong or exploit a compatriot:

because the Lord is an avenger in all these things, just as we have already told you beforehand and solemnly warned you. For God did not call us to impurity but in holiness. Therefore whoever rejects this rejects not human authority but God, who also gives his Holy Spirit to you (4.6-8).

It may be that there is a specific yet unnamed infraction behind the comments here, such as men visiting prostitutes (as seems to be the case in Corinth; see 1 Cor. 6.15-18) or a situation of adultery. Yet, the writers are less focused on the implications for individual morality and point instead to the impact on the collective group ethos. Any individual defilement is a defilement of the group, and thus there is embedded here a charge to the group to be self-regulating in ensuring the integrity of relationships. This emphasis on community wellbeing leads the writers to address another issue of community interaction in the next section of the letter.

Working in the Shadows (4.9-12)

The opening phrase of this section—'now concerning'—is the clearest indication in the letter that the Thessalonians have raised an issue with the Paul party. The Greek construction (*peri de*) is the equivalent of the modern abbreviation 're:', with which we preface remarks responding to some previously raised concern. The Thessalonians must have asked the Paul party to clarify what they meant when they instructed them to practise 'brotherly love' (*philadelphia*). In their response, the writers note, 'you do not need to have anyone write to you, for you yourselves have been taught by God to love one another; and indeed you do love all the brothers and sisters throughout Macedonia' (4.9-10a). Once again, the members of the Thessalonike Christ group are affirmed in what they are already doing and only urged to 'do so more and more' (4.10b).

In this affirmation, the writers seem to coin a new term—'God-taught' (*theodidaktos*). This term has not been found in any ancient Greek writings prior to the time of Paul. There is a similar word, however, that does occur in the writings of the Jewish philosopher Philo. Roetzel (1986) points out that Philo refers to Jews being 'self-taught' (*autodidaktos*) when it comes to taking care of one another. By changing this notion slightly to 'God-taught' the writers of 1 Thessalonians are making explicit what was only implied in Philo's term: God has provided the directive for community members to care for one another. This same term also separates the brotherly love the Christ adherents would have for one another from the brotherly love exemplified between the divine twins Castor and Polydeuces (the Dioscuri). They are known to have had popular appeal within the civic cults of Roman Thessalonike and could be a paradigm for imitation (Kloppenborg 1993). Yet, by insisting that the Christ followers are 'God-taught' the letter writers underscore their audience's separation from all other gods, thus affirming their having turned from gods to God (cf. 1.9).

The question and response about 'brotherly love' has as its focus internal group relationships, but the letter writers continue on to offer a bit of advice that focuses on relationships beyond the group (cf. Burke 2003: 203-24). Again, this advice gives us a picture of the nature of the community, or at least how the letter writers envision the Christ group interacting with outsiders: '[We urge you…] to aspire to live quietly, to mind your own affairs, and to work with your hands, as we directed you, so that you may behave properly toward outsiders and be dependent on no one' (4.11-12). Most associations in antiquity would do anything except aim for a quiet life and self-sufficiency, so much so that this little piece of advice may even be constructed as a direct counter to the usual association practices. In the inscriptions set up by a considerable number of associations we find reference to 'love of honour', the Greek word for which is *philotimia*. A typical example can be seen in this text, taken from a much longer inscription from Athens, which honours the man who founded a group of Soteriasts (literally, 'Saviorists') and went on to be their treasurer and then priest:

> For good fortune, it was resolved by the association of the Soteriasts, whose head of the club is Diodoros son of Sokrates of Aphidna, to commend Diodoros son of Sokrates of Aphidna and to crown him with an olive wreath on account of the love of honour [*philotimia*] that he has continually shown for the association. He is to be crowned yearly by whoever happens to be the treasurer in the same way that the priests and the head of the club are crowned. There shall be a proclamation, that 'the association of the Soterasts crowns Diodoros in accordance with this decision'. This decision shall be inscribed on a monument and set up in the sacred enclosure of Soteira, so that when these things have been completed, all members might be zealous to enhance the association, seeing that its founder obtained a fitting token of good will and a memorial (*GRA* I 48, 37–35 BCE).

The writers of 1 Thessalonians use the same root word, *philotimia*, in their advice to the Christ group, but they subvert it: *philotimeisthai hesychazein*, which can be rendered 'to have love of honour through remaining quiet'. Unlike the association of Soteriasts, in the Thessalonian group there is not to be any crowning, proclamations or presumably inscriptions. Their manner of enhancing the group is not through public display but through their quiet life.

This is striking advice in light of the praise the Thessalonians received in 1 Thessalonians 1 for spreading the news about the work of the Paul party among them and the benefits of allegiance to the one true God. Yet the focus in 1 Thessalonians 4 is of a different sort. It is not a recommendation to be silent about their God. The writers provide some context that frames how such quiet aspirations would appear. The Thessalonians are to do things for themselves and to work with their hands, presumably continuing to earn regular income at their jobs, and they are to treat outsiders with honesty and not rely on anyone for their needs. This latter advice is not simply about self-sufficiency and the so-called 'Protestant work ethic'. It is, once again, a direct counter-cultural move on the part of the letter writers.

The 'zeal for honour' motivated wealthy persons to donate money to the associations, money that would be used for banquets and burials. The money did not need to be repaid, but it did come with strings attached. The wealthy patrons wanted their donations to be acknowledged in a very public way, often through loud proclamations and the setting up of inscriptions and even statues. Again, a few examples can illustrate the type of proclamations that associations made on behalf of their patrons, such as this late first-century CE inscription from Thyatira, found on a marble base that presumably held a statue of the honouree:

> The leather-cutters honored T. Flavius Alexandros son of Metrophanes of the tribe of Quirina, who was market-overseer in a vigorous and extravagant manner for six months, curator of the association of Romans, ambassador to the emperor in Rome three times, legal representative in the laborious cases concerning the Attaleians [?] at his own expense, and priest of Artemis in a manner displaying piety and love of honour [*philotimōs*]. This was set up on behalf of Flavia Alexandra and Flavia Glykinne, his daughters (*AGRW* 131).

Alexandros is recognized as having expended a considerable amount of his own money not only as the market-overseer but also in order to provide ambassadorial and legal representation, along with his role as priest of Artemis. The connection between 'love of honour' and patronage is seen even more clearly in the following inscription, set up by devotees of the God Dionysos Breiseus in first century Smyrna:

> For good fortune! The sacred association of Breiseans honored C. Julius Cheirisophos, son of the literary expert C. Julius Mousonios, who has displayed love of honor [*philotimōs*] in serving as director of contests (*AGRW* 189).

As 'director of the contests', Cheirisophos would have had considerable out of pocket expenses to ensure the games were conducted efficiently and at no cost to the association. In the eyes of the letter writers, the Thessalonian group must act differently when it comes to patrons. While it is fine to proclaim the benefits that come through allegiance to God and brokered through the Paul party, it is not acceptable to seek out patrons who will provide funding in exchange for public honours.

The picture that emerges from 1 Thess. 4.9-12 is that of a workers' association that expresses deep concern and care for one another, but does not seek to draw attention to themselves by getting involved in the machinations of benefaction. They work hard in order to earn enough money, not only to take care of their daily needs but also to fund occasional social get-togethers and the burial of members who pass away. This latter issue, however, has created quite some consternation for the Christ group members, who have expressed some deep doubts and concerns to the Paul party, who respond at length in the final, and lengthiest, section of the body of the letter.

Apocalypse When? (4.13–5.11)

All mortals can be assured of one thing in life—it will end. Reflections on what happens at and after death has been the source of much speculation and fear throughout human history as men and women have struggled to come to grips with their own mortality. This was no less true in the Greco-Roman world, where we have ample evidence of people attempting to prolong their life as much as possible. Compared to the life expectancy in the industrialized West in the twenty-first century, life in the first century was very short. Men tended to live longer than women, perhaps reaching their forties, but it was the exceptional man that lived longer than that. Any number of diseases, accidents or infections could take a man's life before he even turned thirty. The same is true for women, except they had the added threat of complications arising from pregnancy and childbirth, so their life expectancy on average was much shorter (for details see Ascough 2009a: 43-49). Children were particularly susceptible, and many who did survive infancy did not live into their teens. In short, death was all around, and those who did live longer buried many of their friends and relatives.

In this broad cultural context, it would be exciting to hear strangers from an eastern land talking about a God who is willing to help humans escape the inevitability of death, since this God will send his son 'who rescues us from the wrath that is coming' (1.10). True, that same God is going to bring about a large-scale conflagration, but to the members of the Christ group, their survival is guaranteed. This scenario is grounded in Jewish apocalyptic thinking, so it would not be familiar to non-Jews. As we noted in Chapter 1, the apocalyptic genre flourished within Judaism from around 200 BCE through 200 CE, continuing thereafter within the Christian tradition. In this literature, deeply symbolic images are used to convey truths about past, present and future events, with the aim of changing the behaviour of those who read or hear the texts.

As apocalyptic literature developed, so too did the Jewish understanding of the afterlife. At first there was a rather ill-defined place called 'Sheol', in which not much seemed to take place. Beginning with the Book of Daniel, however, writers started to reflect on some 'what if' questions about death. In the last chapter of Daniel, composed in the second century BCE, the writer describes a vision of some of the dead arising from the ground, some reanimated 'to everlasting life, and some to shame and ever-lasting contempt' (Dan. 12.2). Earlier in the book, the writer describes a vision of 'one like a human being ['Son of Man'] coming with the clouds of heaven' (7.13). Such images were developed in subsequent writings, such as *1 Enoch* or the *Testament of Moses*, and by the first century CE there were quite a number of such texts available. Even if they were not read by the majority of Jews, the basic contours of apocalyptic thinking seem to have been widely known, and many Jewish groups expected a messianic saviour to usher in a new world order in the name of God.

Non-Jews did not have such a rich heritage of apocalyptic reflection, and in many instances the literary texts and gravestones suggest that a person simply ceased to exist at death, or at best was transferred to Hades, a shad-owy place of dubious reputation. This is not to suggest, however, that all non-Jews lacked a conception of the afterlife, although it was muted in comparison to Jews. Some gravestones suggest a hope for life beyond death with inscriptions that look forward to reunification in the next life, as did a few philosophical texts (Davies 1999: 135-37). Some of the mysteries imported from Greek traditions, such as that of Dionysos, did hold out some promise of post-mortem continuation (see Graf and Johnston 2007). For the most part, however, during the Roman period there was very little hope for life beyond the grave (Davies 1999: 129), and the best one could look for-ward to was being remembered fondly by friends and family.

Burial practices within any given cultural context can help histori-ans determine how a particular group of people thought about death. We noted earlier that one of the benefits on offer in many of the associations in the Greco-Roman period is the promise of a decent burial. In such cases, deceased members were recalled through the setting up of gravestones, such as these examples set up by occupational associations in Thessalonike:

> The association of Aphrodite Epiteuxidia set this up as a memorial for Athenion son of Praxiteles of Amastris, who has died while abroad. This was set up through their supervisors. Farewell! So also will you be some-time! (*AGRW* 49, 90–91 CE).

> The association of Heron Aulonites set this up for Gaius Julius Crescens. The associates of the head of the gathering [*archisynagōgos*], Artemon the yoke-maker, and the priest, Tryphon, paid for this from what comes from the common chest as a memorial for him (*AGRW* 54, 159/160 CE).

> The association of purple dyers of the eighteenth street honored Menippos, son of Amios, also called Severus, from Thyatira as a memorial (*AGRW* 55, late second century CE).

In a number of cases, burial by an association also included commemora-tions on the anniversary of either the birth or the death of the deceased, or at other points in the calendar year. Such commemorations might be as simple as a request for decorating a grave with crowns, such as was made to an association of sign-bearers by a husband and wife, who provided funds for this to take place twice a year (*IHierapJ* 153, Hierapolis, sometime between 138 and 300 CE). On the other hand, they might involve holding a banquet, as we see in this inscription, from first-century Thessalonike, that stipulates that an association of initiates into the cult of Zeus Dionysos Gongylos will use the income from vineyards donated to them by the deceased:

> to hold a banquet of bread for the supporters, according to the tradition and the donation, on the nineteenth of the month of Dystros, on the thirteenth of the month of Daisios, and on the twenty-third of the month of Gorpiaios. The current and future initiates also swear by the god, by the rites, and by the midnight bread to maintain the above ritual according to the bequest (*AGRW* 50).

The association is to hold three separate banquets in which the donor will be remembered.

Returning to the text of 1 Thessalonians, it is clear from the writers' response that there is a problem around 'those who have died' among the Thessalonian Christ group (5.13). The precise nature of the problem is, however, far from clear and has generated quite some discussion among commentators, who attempt to construct the issue from the answer that is provided (summarized well in Luckensmeyer 2009: 18-40). My own view is that the problem reflected in this text really is one of community belonging that can best be understood in light of the types of responses to death we see in other groups, such as the association texts quoted above (Ascough 2004; 2011a). The grieving and loss of hope that the writers address reflect the dismay on the part of the Thessalonian Christ group members that the premature death of some of their members precludes them from being 'caught up in the clouds' (4.17) when Jesus returns. Because they have died, they are no longer a part of the living community that God will save 'from the coming wrath' (1.10) at the return of Jesus.

Whereas normally the group would have performed the rituals of burial for their deceased member, and perhaps even incorporated their memory into the established pattern of group commemoration such as an annual banquet, after they changed their allegiance to this new God they assumed there no longer would be any need to do so. When a few of their members subsequently passed away, they were puzzled. If Paul and his companions had preached a message similar to that found in other letters, namely that death is the result of sin (1 Cor. 15.56; Rom. 5.12), then the Thessalonians might have concluded that the recently departed members had been separated from the group through sin. This would be all the more reason to disassociate from them and not undertake any sort of memorial commemoration on their behalf. It truly would be a loss of hope—loss of hope that the deceased would be saved at the coming of Jesus, and perhaps even loss of hope that Jesus would come at all.

Quite the contrary is the case, declare the letter writers: 'we do not want you to be uninformed, brothers and sisters, about those who have died, so that you may not grieve as others do who have no hope' (4.13). In fact, the letter writers do not even use the Greek word for 'died', despite the translation of the NRSV. Instead, they use a metaphor to open this passage: 'those who are asleep' (4.13, 14). It is as if to say, they are not separated from the community because of sin, or because of any other reason. At the coming of Jesus they will arise first, joined mid-air by those who do not 'sleep'. Here, however, they drop the metaphor, explicitly recognizing that these members have died physically: 'the dead in Christ will rise first. Then we who are alive, who are left, will be caught up in the clouds together with them to meet the Lord in the air' (4.16b-17). Through this assurance, the writers help the Thessalonians forge and solidify their communal identity (cf. Luckensmeyer 2009: 326) and recognize that the death of some members is not inconsistent with the message first proclaimed by the Paul party (Pahl 2009: 153-55).

The death of some members seems also to have occasioned another question on the part of the members of the Christ group in Thessalonike, namely, when will Jesus return? They are understandably becoming impatient, particularly if they think they too may die before the event and thus miss out on all the benefits they assume come through allegiance to God. The opening *peri de* formula in 5.1 indicates that again the writers are addressing an issue raised by the Thessalonians: 'Now concerning the times and the seasons, brothers and sisters...' Curiously, although the writers immediately claim 'you do not need to have anything written to you', they go on to employ a couple of examples to reassure the Thessalonians that Jesus' descent from the heavens could occur at any moment, completely without warning. The two examples do make the point of something happening unexpectedly, but they have struck commentators as odd. The first example involves robbery: 'the day of the Lord will come like a thief in the night' (5.2, an image also used in 1 Pet. 3.10). In this case, although theft does come by surprise, it is not inevitable in the same way the writers indicate the return of Jesus will definitely come. The second example is inevitable, but it lacks the same kind of surprise: 'as labor pains come upon a pregnant woman' (5.3). In this instance, while one cannot predict precisely when labour will begin, there is a very limited range, and it certainly will take place within a nine-month period or so.

Other language in this passage does not fit well either. A complacent sigh of 'peace and security' is contrasted with the 'destruction' of childbirth. Yet the latter is about bringing life, not meting out destruction, although the writers are correct that there is no escaping childbirth for the pregnant woman involved. The real point, however, is that events will unfold quickly, and we should not attempt to over-interpret the metaphors employed. The writers assure the Thessalonians that although Jesus will indeed appear, the timing can never be known. As a result, constant vigilance is required. Yet this should not engender fear or uncertainty (5.8), but continued hope and concern for one another: 'Therefore encourage one another and build up each other, as indeed you are doing' (5.11). Once again we see the writers both urging solidarity and, at the same time, assuring the members of the Thessalonian Christ group that they are indeed already undertaking such. This is, it seems, a strongly unified community.

Despite a lot of academically sound scholarship, the history of interpretation of 1 Thessalonians 4.13–5.11 is fraught with wild speculation about end of the world scenarios. The passage is often woven together with texts from elsewhere in the New Testament and the Hebrew Bible, particularly Daniel and the Book of Revelation. Yet the key concern in this passage is not to set out systematically the events or timing of the return of Jesus but to address a pastoral concern within the group to which they write. The members have lost hope, which the writers want to restore. In a subsequent letter, this time addressed to the Christ group at Corinth, Paul and Sosthenes will present a series of similar descriptors, elaborating them only somewhat, and changing them slightly (1 Cor. 15.51-57). Yet the differences in the Pauline letters, along with the often vast distinctions between the Pauline eschatological view and that of Revelation, suggest that the metaphoric language was not meant to be pieced together like a grand puzzle that reveals the end of the world. More could be said on this, but space does not permit. We will not, however, completely leave behind the topic of eschatology because it looms large in 2 Thessalonians, the letter to which we now turn our attention.

Writing with Authority—2 Thessalonians

Our construction of the nature of the Thessalonian community thus far has been grounded in interpretations of 1 Thessalonians within the socio-cultural context of the Greco-Roman world. The canonical letter we refer to as 2 Thessalonians has, quite deliberately, been left to one side in our picture. At this point, however, we do need to give it some attention and, as we will see, it becomes a complicating factor, largely due to questions around its authenticity. Not all scholars agree that Paul and his companions wrote this letter; instead, they argue that it was sent to the Thessalonian Christ group at some later date. If this is the case, then 2 Thessalonians gives us a picture of the group in the second or even third generation of its existence. In and of itself, this is very interesting because we can track some developments within the community. Other equally reputable scholars, however, maintain that it is a letter written by Paul, Silvanus and Timothy, just as it claims in 1.1. In this case, it gives us further information concerning the Thessalonian Christ group shortly after they received the first letter. That said, there are a couple of scholars who do agree that the letter is authentic, but argue that it was sent to Thessalonike before 1 Thessalonians, and thus gives us a picture of the community at an even earlier stage, before some of the developments referred to in our chapters above.

In the first section of this chapter we will consider these options and the scholars that maintain these positions. In the following two sections we will consider the structure of the letter and the rhetorical argumentation of the letter, much as we did for 1 Thessalonians. As a result of all of these considerations we will, at the end, be in a position to draw some preliminary conclusions on the issue of how and where 2 Thessalonians fits into an historical reconstruction of the Christ group at Thessalonike.

A Letter 'as though from us' (2 Thess. 2.2)

In seeking to assure the Thessalonians around the return of Jesus, the letter writers note, 'we beg you, brothers and sisters, not to be quickly shaken in mind or alarmed, either by spirit or by word or by letter, as though from us, to the effect that the day of the Lord is already here' (2.2). This is a clear indication that there were letters circulating among Christ groups that bore the names of Paul and his companions but were not really written by them. Letters or other documents written in the name of someone other than the actual author are called pseudonymous texts, that is, texts that carry a false name (mostly, the name of a famous person). Quite a number of these works are known from antiquity, such as works bearing the name of Plato (e.g. *Sisyphus*; *Axiochus*) or Aristotle (e.g. *Economics*; *On the Universe*), but most likely written and preserved by their respective followers. Much of the early non-canonical Christian literature claims prominent followers of Jesus as their authors, such as the *Gospel of Thomas* or the *Protoevangelium of James*.

Even Paul is credited with authorship of two non-canonical letters—Laodiceans and 3 Corinthians—that do not cohere with the authentic Pauline letters in terms of the language used, the theology assumed and the historical situations presupposed (see Soards 1988: 206-207 for details). There also exists a series of letters exchanged between Paul and the Roman philosopher Seneca, who like Paul was alive during the first half of the first century CE (c. 4 BCE to 65 CE), but these letters again are clearly not authentic on both sides of the exchange.

This Christian evidence comes from the second century or later and demonstrates that at least some early Christians were willing to produce letters in the name of Paul and others were willing to circulate and read them. The inspiration for doing so likely comes from some references in the canonical letters that mention letters of Paul that are now lost, such as those written to Corinth (1 Cor. 1.9) or to Laodicea (Col. 4.15-16). It is unlikely there was a deliberate attempt to be duplicitous. Early Christians writing in the name of Paul probably viewed their actions as honouring Paul and preserving his apostolic teaching, even while they drew upon his authority to address situations in their own community contexts. The question, remains, however, as to whether 2 Thessalonians itself is one such letter and, if so, should it be dated to the early second century (or later) as are the other forged Pauline letters, or is it an earlier pseudonymous letter. One way to decide is to look at the letter itself.

The letter opens with a greeting from the same triad that composed 1 Thessalonians: Paul, Silvanus and Timothy. Among the Paul party they are presumably the most significant contacts for the Thessalonians. Towards the end of the letter, Paul interjects his own voice: 'I, Paul, write this greeting with my own hand. This is the mark in every letter of mine; it is the way I write' (3.17). He has thus signed the letter with his own hand as a means of authenticating it, a practice mentioned in three other Pauline letters, all of them whose authorship is not disputed:

- 'I, Paul, write this greeting with my own hand' (1 Cor. 16.21);
- 'See what large letters I make when I am writing in my own hand!' (Gal. 6.11);
- 'I, Paul, am writing this with my own hand: I will repay it' (Phlm 19).

Notice, however, that in none of these three cases is the greeting used as a means to authenticate the letter. Some scholars suggest that the writer of 2 Thessalonians 'doth protest too much' and that this is a signal that the letter is forged. Although it is meant to reassure the readers that the letter is genuine (in contrast to the letter mentioned in 2.2), it is equally forged.

The signature itself would be inconsequential, since it would be easy enough to claim at a later date that the actual papyrus in the possession of the Thessalonians was simply a copy of the original; many such copies were made for wider distribution, especially in the late first and early second century. Thus, we can conjecture a later writer addressing a situation in which there was false information circulating under the names of Paul and his companions concerning the events around Jesus' return. Such false rumours had upset the Christ group members at Thessalonike, and in order to calm and assure them, the leaders 'found' a letter from Paul, Silvanus and Timothy that lays out the correct understanding of what must take place, while also addressing some other pressing concerns affecting the group. Paul's authority was thus invoked on both issues, but in the latter case with the imprimatur of the leadership team. This scenario is possible, but quite conjectural, and the evidence for and against the authenticity of 2 Thessalonians is still quite flimsy. Hence, we must continue our investigation.

Over 100 years ago William Wrede (1903) argued against the authenticity of 2 Thessalonians on the basis of a number of factors such as vocabulary, style, content and theology, positing a post-70 CE date for its composition, even suggesting it be dated to the early second century (although he was not the first to doubt the authenticity of 2 Thessalonians; see Wanamaker 1990: 17-19). This provided the foundation for the debate that has continued since that time, with commentators expanding on one or more aspects in various ways, as well as drawing on new methods of research. One of the most thorough attempts to assess the evidence came with the appearance of Wolfgang Trilling's German monograph on the subject (1972) in which he mounts three arguments against the authenticity of 2 Thessalonians. Commentators since that time have either built on Trilling to argue against the letter's authenticity, or refuted Trilling in order to maintain its authenticity. Wanamaker is a case in point; he provides perhaps one of the best comprehensive summary and critique of Trilling's position in his commentary (1990: 21-28).

One of Trilling's main arguments focused on the appearance of unusual expressions in 2 Thessalonians, listing 40 of these and concluding that although they do not themselves confirm non-Pauline authorship, they do point to a shift in thinking, particularly in how the writers discuss apocalyptic themes. Yet, as Wanamaker points out, a shift in the nature of the subject itself is sufficient to warrant a shift in vocabulary; there is no need to posit a different author (1990: 21). In addition, every letter bearing the name of Paul has a list of unique expressions, yet this does not give rise to questions of the authorship of letters such as Romans or 1 Corinthians. There is no reason to expect 2 Thessalonians to be any different in presenting so unique a vocabulary.

In a similar vein, Collins (1990a) notes that there are some Pauline terms that are not used anywhere in 2 Thessalonians, such as 'preach', 'gospel', 'love', 'sin' and 'apostle'; this is striking as they are key to Pauline arguments in the undisputed letters (Romans, 1 and 2 Corinthians, Galatians, Philippians, 1 Thessalonians and Philemon). Arguments from silence, however, are seldom convincing in and of themselves, and counter propositions can be made. For example, the differences in vocabulary can be explained by the length of the letter, or the limited focus, or the use of a secretary, who was given a bit of a free hand in writing down what was dictated to him, as was sometimes the practice in antiquity. As it happens, more than three quarters of the vocabulary in 2 Thessalonians can be found in the authentic Pauline letters, thus suggesting they share common authorship. But in the case of 'on the one hand…on the other hand', this same statistic can be used to argue that it is a forgery, because a good forger would model his or her style on letters written by the person(s) that is being emulated. Round and round the argument about vocabulary continues, with no conclusion in sight.

Another of Trilling's primary arguments focused on stylistic features of 2 Thessalonians. On a very simple level, the letter contains sentences that are longer than those found in the undisputed Pauline letters. But Trilling took it further to show that the use of stylistic features such as parallelism, metaphors, chiastic structures and such pale in comparison to the style used in 1 Thessalonians. Once again, however, this may be explained by altered circumstances or the use of a secretary without necessarily detracting from the substance of the letter coming from Paul and his companions. This also may explain the supposed lack of warmth or personal tone that some commentators suggest demarcate 2 Thessalonians (Bailey 1978/1979).

Schmidt (1990) undertakes a somewhat different stylistic analysis by focusing on syntactical features to show that 2 Thessalonians bears closer similarity to Colossians and Ephesians than other letters considered authentically Pauline, including 1 Thessalonians. Given his position that Colossians and Ephesians are not among the authentic letters, the syntactical similarities with 2 Thessalonians puts the latter in the same category. The argument is slightly circular, however, since it relies on Colossians and

Ephesians being deemed inauthentic on grounds that often include syntactical considerations. If one disagrees with this conclusion and decides that Colossians and Ephesians are authentic, then the similarities that 2 Thessalonians share with them would deem that it too is authentic.

The linguistic and stylistic arguments are often very technical and not without merit for exploring the meaning in the texts, but ultimately have proved inconclusive in and of themselves on the issue of authenticity. In the end, 2 Thessalonians is too brief and the collection of Pauline letters too small to provide a dataset of vocabulary and syntactical style of the depth that is necessary to undertake meaningful analysis. It is simply not possible to solve the question of authorship on the basis of language and style alone and other features of the letter must be considered.

Receiving the Letter

There is very little argument among scholars concerning the compositional unity of 2 Thessalonians, which is to say that there is no identifiable section that might be an interpolation, nor anywhere that a section seems to have gone missing. It is shorter than most other canonical letters ascribed to Paul, the exceptions being Titus and Philemon. Like almost all the other letters, it follows the epistolary conventions of Greco-Roman letters of opening, thanksgiving, body, closing. There is general agreement among commentators on the extent of the letter opening (1.1-2), thanksgiving (1.3-12) and closing (3.16-18), but some debate over how best to divide the body of the letter. While some commentators argue that the letter body extends to 3.15, others note the presence of a second thanksgiving section at 2.13–3.5 and the nature of the material in 3.6-15, which seems to some like the moral exhortation of a letter. This certainly would be in keeping with the format in other Pauline letters, including 1 Thessalonians. Thus, we can outline the flow of the letter according to the format:

1.1-2	Letter opening, in which the writers and the recipients are identified.
1.3-12	Thanksgiving section in which the writers highlight the positive aspects of the recipients and wish them well.
2.1-12	The body of the letter in which the writers reassure the Thessalonians concerning the timing of the coming of Jesus.
2.13–3.5	A second thanksgiving, in which God's faithfulness is affirmed.
3.6-15	The *paraenesis*, general exhortations, in which the writers address issues of behaviour disruptive to the group.
3.16-18	Letter closing, including final greetings.

We noted in the previous section that 2 Thessalonians is similar in structure to 1 Thessalonians, which is not surprising in the sense that both follow the standard letter format of antiquity. There is one curious piece, however, in that both letters include two thanksgiving sections, with the second one placed well into or after the body of the letter (1 Thess. 2.13-16 and 2 Thess. 2.13–3.5). In Chapter 2 we noted that this feature is among the reasons many commentators think that 1 Thess. 2.13-16 is an interpolation, particularly given that the content does not fit the literary or historical context. In the case of the second thanksgiving in 2 Thessalonians, the content of the second thanksgiving is unproblematic. Its presence, however, suggests to some that a later writer has copied the format of 1 Thessalonians. While it might be argued that the same writers of both letters chose to include the unusual second thanksgiving, we have no other example of a Pauline letter in which this happens.

In and of itself this does not offer conclusive evidence for the use of 1 Thessalonians as a model for the writing of 2 Thessalonians. There are other places, however, where the wording and structure of the second letter parallels the first, outlined in the following chart, with the similarities in wording underlined:

	1 Thessalonians	*2 Thessalonians*
Prescript	1.1 <u>Paul, Silvanus, and Timothy, to the church of the Thessalonians</u> in God the Father <u>and the Lord Jesus Christ:</u> <u>Grace to you and peace.</u>	1.1-2 <u>Paul, Silvanus, and Timothy, To the church of the Thessalonians</u> in God our Father <u>and the Lord Jesus Christ: Grace to you and peace</u> from God our Father and the Lord Jesus Christ.
Thanksgiving	1.2 <u>We always give thanks to God for</u> all of <u>you</u>…	1.3 <u>We</u> must <u>always give thanks to God for you</u>, brothers…
Benediction	3.11-13 <u>Now may our God</u> and Father <u>himself</u> and <u>our Lord Jesus</u> direct our way to you. And may the Lord make you increase and abound in love for one another and for all, just as we abound in love for you. And may he so <u>strengthen your hearts</u> in holiness that you may be blameless before our God and Father at the coming of our Lord Jesus with all his saints.	2.16-17 Now may <u>our Lord Jesus Christ himself</u> and <u>God our Father</u>, who loved us and through grace gave us eternal comfort and good hope, comfort <u>your hearts</u> and <u>strengthen</u> them in every good work and word.
Adverb of conclusion	4.1 <u>Finally, brothers,</u> we ask and urge you in the Lord Jesus…	3.1 <u>Finally, brothers,</u> pray for us…

Moral Exhortation (*Paraenesis*)	5.14 And we urge you, brothers, to admonish the <u>idlers,</u> encourage the faint hearted, help the weak, be patient with all of them.	3.6 Now we command you, brothers, in the name of our Lord Jesus Christ, to keep away from believers who are <u>living in idleness</u> and not according to the tradition that they received from us.
Peace Wish	5.23-24 <u>May the</u> God of <u>peace himself</u> sanctify you entirely; and may your spirit and soul and body be kept sound and blameless at the coming of our Lord Jesus Christ.	3.16 Now <u>may the</u> Lord <u>of peace himself</u> give you peace at all times in all ways.
Prayer Request	5.25 <u>brothers, pray for us.</u>	3.1 <u>brothers, pray for us,</u> so that the word of the Lord may spread rapidly and be glorified everywhere, just as it is among you,
Greetings	5.26 <u>Greet</u> all the brothers and sisters with a holy kiss. Solemnly command you by the Lord that this letter be read to all of them.	3.17 I, Paul, write this <u>greeting</u> with my own hand. This is the mark in every letter of mine; it is the way I write.
Benediction	5.28 <u>The grace of our Lord Jesus Christ be with you.</u>	3.18 <u>The grace of our Lord Jesus Christ be with</u> all of <u>you.</u>

Most of these parallels are found in the opening and closing of the letter, which are places that are broad and general and thus one might expect to find some repetition by the same writers composing a letter to the same community. In addition, the overlap in content and vocabulary is very general and some of it can be found in other Pauline letters, such as the language of 'grace' and 'peace' in the opening greeting (see Rom. 1.7, 1 Cor. 1.1, 2 Cor. 1.1, Gal. 1.1, Phil. 1.2, and Phlm 3). In other instances, although there is broad similarity the content is different, such as the general prayer request of 1 Thess. 5.25 and the very specific requests made in 2 Thess. 3.1. In addition, within the similarities, there are also marked differences, such as the addition of the words 'from God the Father and the Lord Jesus Christ' to the opening greeting. This is also the case in the closing, which includes a directive for public reading of the letter and a holy kiss in 1 Thess. 5.27, whereas 2 Thess. 3.17 has a personalized greeting from Paul. All of this serves to convince many commentators that the similarities can best be explained by positing that Paul, Silvanus and Timothy composed both Thessalonian letters.

Nevertheless, when other commentators take note of these parallel features of the two Thessalonian letters, along with aspects typical of other

Pauline compositions, they maintain that it is in the opening and closing of a letter that a forger would find it easiest to imitate the style and language of an original while still making his own modifications. Combined with the inclusion of a second thanksgiving section in both letters, they argue that someone other than Paul has crafted 2 Thessalonians using 1 Thessalonians, and perhaps other Pauline letters, as an exemplar. Yet again we find that the evidence for or against 2 Thessalonians being authentic has proven inconclusive among commentators, so we must continue to look for evidence by turning our attention to the flow of the letter.

Reading the Letter

As we noted in Chapter 2 with reference to 1 Thessalonians, much scholarly attention has been devoted to identifying the rhetorical species of Pauline letters according to the ancient types of judicial, deliberative and epideictic rhetoric. The aim of so doing is to determine how the letter writers are attempting to persuade their audience through their use of language. As was the case with 1 Thessalonians, there is no basic agreement among commentators as to where these rhetorical divisions lie within the letter, as the following chart shows:

	Prescriptio	Exordium	Narratio	Partitio	Probatio	Peroratio	Exhortatio	Closing
Donfried 1993	-	1.1-12	-	2.1-2	2.3-13	2.16-18	3.1-15	3.16-17
Holland 1988	1.1-2	1.3-4	1.5-12	-	2.1-17	3.14-16	3.1-13	3.17-18
Hughes 1989	-	1.1-12	-	2.1-2	2.3-15	2.16-17	3.1-15	3.16-18
Jewett 1986	-	1.1-12	-	2.1-2	2.3-3.5	3.16-18	3.6-15	-
Wanamaker 1990	1.1-2	1.3-12	-	2.1-2	2.3-15	2.16-17	3.1-15	3.16-18

Not surprisingly, where the significant disagreement in the rhetorical divisions lie is how best to sort the text from 2.1 through 3.15; this section is also the challenge for those who attempted to divide the letter according to epistolary conventions, although those noted above all see 3.1-15 constituting the *exhortatio*, with the exception of Jewett who begins it at 3.6. The outlier in this is Witherington (2006), who divides the letter quite differently and introduces a number of non-standard rhetorical categories intermixed with epistolary designations: prescript (1.1-2), *exordium* (1.3-10), *proposition* (1.11-12), *refutatio* (2.1-2), thanks (2.13-15), *transitus* (2.16-17), final request (3.1-5), *probatio* (3.6-12), *peroratio* (3.13-15), *exhortatio* (3.6-12), closing (3.16-18). His schema has not received general acceptance, in part because there seems to be little gained by such minute divisions.

Despite these differences in rhetorical divisions, almost all commentators agree that the rhetoric of the letter can be categorized as deliberative,
insofar as it attempts to convince a somewhat critical audience of the advan-
tages of a recommended course of action and argue that to do otherwise
would produce disadvantages. That said, the attempt to classify the species of rhetoric in 2 Thessalonians and to identify each rhetorical division
falls upon the same problems discussed with respect to the same interpretive strategy applied to 1 Thessalonians. It reflects an outmoded belief that
letters are replacements for the physical presence of the writer and should
thus be read in the vein of 'here's the speech I would give if I was standing among you'. This is simply not the case, and the oral and written performative aspects of the text must be subject to a much more sophisticated
socio-rhetorical analysis, of the sort we noted in Chapter 2 that is being
undertaken by the members of the Rhetoric of Religious Antiquity project.

In 2 Thessalonians, there are three areas of concern, each of which we
will examine in detail in the next chapter: the need to reduce anxiety concerning the coming of Jesus (2.1-12), the need to remain faithful, particularly in the face of external opposition (1.3-12 and 2.13–3.5), and the need
to contain members who are disrupting group meetings (3.6-15). Underlying the writers' response to each is the theological conviction that God is
faithful to those who believe (3.3-5) and thus those who believe must remain
committed and loyal to God (2.15). Unfortunately, however, we still are not
yet in a position to draw a definitive conclusion on whether 2 Thessalonians
is an original composition of Paul and his companions or a later imitation,
albeit one with good intentions that not only draws on Paul's authority but
also reveres his memory (Holland 1990). That said, it clearly does reflect
the Pauline style and contains themes consistent with other letters in the
New Testament that are considered authentically Pauline. Together the style
and language are presented in such a way as to bring hope to those experiencing abuse from outsiders and disruptions from within, as well as, most
significantly, to those who are distressed because of the ambiguity and fear
surrounding the timing of the coming of Jesus. The writers emphasize that
God is faithful to those who believe, and thus the believers must remain
faithful to God in the face of abuse, disruption and distress.

For many scholars, it is this latter issue, particularly distress over the
timing of Jesus' return and the response of the letter writers, that is crucial
to making a decision about whether or not 2 Thessalonians was written by
the same committee that composed 1 Thessalonians. The key is whether the
timing and events presented in 2 Thessalonians can be reconciled with those
of 1 Thessalonians, despite a few differences. If so, then the authorship is
shared between the two letters. If not, that is, if there are significant and
somewhat irreconcilable differences in the schemas, then it becomes more
likely that 2 Thessalonians was written at a later date by different hands in

order to address different circumstances. Thus, before we can make a final decision concerning the authenticity of 2 Thessalonians we must consider the evidence from the letter itself regarding these three concerns. This we will do in Chapter 6, by again giving attention to the intersection of rhetorical strategies and cultural references as a way to gauge the impact that the writers were attempting to have through their letter.

ADJUSTING FOR NEW CIRCUMSTANCES

In this chapter we will look at three issues the letter writers discuss in 2 Thessalonians. The opening thanksgiving section of the letter notes that the Thessalonian Christ followers are undergoing significant suffering at the hands of their enemies. The writers seek to bolster their perseverance by assuring them that God is with them (1.3-12), a move repeated in the second thanksgiving section (2.13–3.5). On top of the trouble at the hands of outsiders, there also exist some problems internal to the community, with some of the adherents creating disturbances and refusing to share in the work that is the basis of the financial support of the community (3.6-15).

The writers' primary concern in writing, however, focuses on correcting some misunderstanding and calming some apprehension around the timing of the coming of Jesus. It is with respect to this issue that we find commentators debating whether or not there is coherence with the content of 1 Thessalonians on the same subject. This is often the place where the question of authorship is settled for or against the same writers for both letters. If there is coherence between 1 and 2 Thessalonians, even if it shows development along the same trajectory, then there is little reason to discount both being written by the same authors. On the other hand, if there is any disjuncture in the description or timing of the events in 2 Thessalonians, we are faced with two possibilities: (1) either the writers of 1 Thessalonians altered their thinking to address changed circumstances within the decade or so between the first composition around 49 CE and the death of Paul around 62 CE (e.g. Jewett 1986; Malherbe 2000; Nicholl 2004; Witherington 2006), or (2) the text was composed by a different writer or writers who were addressing changed circumstances for a different generation (e.g. Hughes 1989; Menken 1994; Richard 1995; Donfried 2002). We will address this issue first and thus be able to draw our own conclusion concerning the authorship of 2 Thessalonians, before turning briefly to the other two issues the letter writers raise in the letter.

Wait, What Now? (2 Thess. 2.1-17)

In Chapter 4 we discussed at some length 1 Thess. 4.13–5.11, where the letter writers address a question raised by the Christ followers in Thessalonike concerning the fate of recently deceased members. The writers assure the group that anyone who has died since they gave their allegiance to God is assured of a place with Jesus in heaven. They describe some of the events that will mark the initial coming of Jesus to gather up the faithful, both those living and those who have died, but go on to note that the timing of this inaugural event is not and cannot be known by anyone. The issue of the characteristics and timing of this inaugural event is taken up again by the writers of 2 Thessalonians, but in response to a different issue. It seems that news has reached the Paul party that there are false rumours, circulating both orally and in writing, that Jesus has already returned. This news has shaken the members of the Thessalonian Christ group, who assume that they have been by-passed in the gathering into the air. If the rumours are true, they must have reasoned, then they have been left behind to experience the coming of God's wrath upon the earth (cf. 1 Thess. 1.10). This may be how they understand the suffering they are presently experiencing. They are understandably 'shaken in mind' and 'alarmed' (2 Thess. 2.1). The writers seek to calm these fears by reviewing the events that must unfold as a means to demonstrate that Jesus has not yet returned. The Thessalonians can rest assured that they have not been left out.

The following chart demonstrates the overlaps in the events that are described in the eschatological schema of each letter, while also highlighting some differences:

1 Thessalonians	*2 Thessalonians*
Day of the Lord (5.2)	Day of the Lord (2.2)
Jesus [coming] out of the heavens (1.10)	The revelation (*apokalypsis*) of Jesus out of heaven (1.7)
The arrival (*parousia*) of the Lord (4.15; cf. 2.19)	The arrival (*parousia*) of the Lord (2.1; 2.8)
Jesus is accompanied by the cry of an archangel, along with a summons and a trumpet blast (4.16)	Jesus is accompanied by powerful angels (1.7) and flaming fire (1.8)
Believers who have died rise up (4.16b)	
Believers still living are snatched up in the clouds (4.17a)	
Dead and alive believers meet Jesus in the air (4.17b)	Believers gather together (*episynagōgē*) with Jesus (2.1)
Believers are always to be with Jesus (4.17)	
Destruction (*olethros*) comes upon those not raised up to be with Jesus (5.3)	Vengeance (*ekdikēsis*) is meted out upon those not knowing God (1.8)
Believers are delivered from the coming wrath (*orgē*, 1.10 and 5.9)	
The time will be marked as one of peace and safety (5.3)	A period of apostasy (2.3a) and a time of delusion (2.11)

The events come unexpectedly (5.3a)—like a 'thief in the night' (5.2, 4) and like birth-pains to a pregnant woman (5.3b)	The time is preceded by the revealing (*apokalyptō*) of 'the lawless one', the 'son of destruction' (2.3b), who claims to be a god and sits in the Temple (2.4b), and demonstrates power, signs and wonders as a manifestation of Satan's activity (2.9)
	Non-believers will be deceived by the activities of 'the lawless one' (2.10)
	The revealing (*apokalyptō*) of 'the lawless one' [for what he really is] and his destruction (*anaireō*) by Jesus (2.8; cf. 2.6)

There is a fair amount of overlap in the schema outlined in each of the letters. Both refer to a 'day of the Lord' being inaugurated by Jesus, whose arrival is described in both letters using the Greek word *parousia*. It is a word that has political implications; it is used in contexts of the arrival of an emperor, an image bolstered in part by the images of what will accompany Jesus: announcements, trumpets and a powerful agent ('archangel') in 1 Thessalonians and powerful agents ('angels') and flaming fire in 2 Thessalonians. Both letters agree that there will be a meeting of believers with Jesus, although 1 Thessalonians provides more detail about the location 'in the air' and the order in which Christ group members will be taken up (the dead first, who are joined *en route* by the living), along with the explicit assurance that this meeting with Jesus is to be a permanent arrangement. Finally, both letters agree that something bad will happen to non-adherents, although 1 Thessalonians adds the assurance that none of this will befall Christ followers.

Although there are slight variations between the two letters, the overall picture described above is similar. One striking difference between the two letters is the omission in 2 Thessalonians of any reference to 'we who are alive, who are left until the coming of the Lord' as there is in 1 Thess. 4.15. In the earlier letter, the writers clearly anticipate that they will still be alive when Jesus comes. In a similar account concerning the coming of Jesus conveyed by Paul and Sosthenes to the Corinthians they again anticipate at least some of those presently alive will remain so until the time of Jesus' arrival: 'We will not all die, but we will all be changed' (1 Cor. 15.51). In 2 Thessalonians, however, there is no such indication of Paul and his companions being alive. While it is not explicitly denied, this absence has suggested to some commentators that the writer or writers of this letter are already aware that Paul and others of the first generation of Christ adherents have passed away.

Where the two letters come into more direct conflict with one another is around the issue of whether the timing of events can be anticipated, particularly the nature of the events that will allow adherents to know that Jesus' *parousia* is about to take place. According to 1 Thessalonians, the coming of Jesus will creep up on the believers in a time marked by peace and safety, and they will be somewhat surprised, as if by a thief or the labour pains of a pregnant women. In 2 Thessalonians, however, there are clear indications that the 'day of the Lord' is about to be inaugurated. Of particular note is the reference to a 'man of lawlessness', who is an agent of Satan, although not Satan himself (2.9).

This exact image is otherwise unknown in the Jewish apocalyptic tradition, although there are depictions of evil figures that oppose God (Harrison 2010: 75-77). A more likely connection, however, is with one of the succession of Roman emperors, who were venerated as gods. Among them some in particular stand out as contenders for the label 'man of lawlessness'. Harrison (2010: 78-95) makes the case for Caligula, who attempted to set up a statue of himself in the Jerusalem Temple in 40 CE. In the later Flavian period, Domitian equally made above average claims to divinity, expanding the imperial cult throughout the empire. Yet attempting to identify one or another specific emperor as the target of the label would fall prey to the kind of interpretation the writers themselves warn against in noting that while the 'lawlessness' is already at work, the identity of 'the man' is yet to be revealed, since at the time of writing he is still under restraint (2 Thess. 2.7).

While we may not be able to identify 'the man of lawlessness', for our purposes what is critical is that the writers indicate that his presence will be known and identifiable preceding the coming of Jesus. At first he will be perceived as a deity, demonstrating power, signs and false marvels, thus deceiving those who do not follow Christ. This is the 'rebellion' (2.3) against God, and as such will be known to the believers. It is a marked difference from a time of complacency in which believers are able to breath a sigh of relief at the 'peace and safety' around them, only to be surprised by the cacophony of trumpets and shouts that proclaim the *parousia* of Jesus, as described in 1 Thessalonians.

In 2 Thessalonians we find the articulation of events that will be known and thus can mark the coming of Jesus: a time of apostasy and delusion in which people reject God (2.3a, 10-12) and the appearance of a 'man of lawlessness' (2.3b-8), who will deceive non-believers through false signs and wonders (2.9). Although he is currently being held back by 'the restrainer', this 'man of lawlessness' will be revealed according to God's timing (2.6). The inclusion of these events in the letter is not meant to incite apocalyptic speculation over the identity of 'the man of lawlessness' nor that of 'the restrainer', although both have been subject of much scholarly and popular speculation throughout Christian history. In contrast, the letter writers are less concerned to provide a precise identification than they are concerned to assuage the Thessalonians' doubt and worry by assuring them that they will know when the time is near and will not be left out. This is a marked difference in the depiction of the unfolding of the events presented in 1 and 2 Thessalonians.

One solution to the issue of the differences in the eschatological chronology is reversing the order of the letters, a solution first proposed in the early seventeenth century by Hugo Grotius, who argued that the inclusion of a greeting by Paul's own hand (2 Thess. 3.17) only made sense if written at the end of the first letter sent to Thessalonike. Thus, Grotius concludes that the canonical order should be reversed, with 2 Thessalonians preceding 1 Thessalonians. Certainly there is no reason to accept the canonical order at face value, since the letters were arranged according to length, not chronology, and the titles 'first' and 'second' were added much later. Although Grotius' position has not met with widespread acceptance, Wanamaker (1990) has taken up the mantle in recent times (also Hurd 1998). Wanamaker argues that the 'present' trouble in 2 Thessalonians is depicted in 1 Thessalonians as already in the past. More importantly, the reason the writers have 'no need' to tell the Thessalonians of the 'times and seasons' pertaining to the coming of Jesus (1 Thess. 5.1) is because they have already outlined the signs in their first letter (2 Thess. 3.12). While this does make some sense of the letters, it does not explain why the writers of 1 Thessalonians would insist on the suddenness of the events when in 2 Thessalonians they sought to show how there would be signs and revelations that would provide fair warning.

Another piece of data against arguments for reversing the letter order is the letter writers' reference in 2 Thess. 2.15 to traditions that the Thessalonians have learned from them 'by our letter'. If 2 Thessalonians precedes 1 Thessalonians, then we have yet another letter to the Thessalonians that came even earlier. While not impossible, it creates a scenario in which the Paul party's sudden departure from Thessalonike has created some consternation among the Christ group members, but this is not addressed in any detail until the third letter that they receive. A three-letter scenario also does not cohere with the urgency Paul and his companions express in 1 Thessalonians around their need to have news of the progress of the community, resulting in their sending Timothy to the city (1 Thess. 2.17, 3.5). While reversing the order of 1 and 2 Thessalonians might alleviate some conflict in the apocalyptic timetable between the two letters, it raises other issues that to my mind are more problematic. Thus, I judge it unlikely that 1 Thessalonians follows 2 Thessalonians in terms of historical order.

We are now perhaps at a point where we can draw together the evidence assessed concerning the authenticity of 2 Thessalonians and make a decision. The following issues, including some preliminary conclusions, have been discussed in some detail in this and the previous chapter:

- linguistic and stylistic arguments show some differences that might suggest different authorship, although overall 2 Thessalonians has a 'Pauline' style;
- there is a marked similarity in the overall structure of the two letters, including the odd inclusion of a second thanksgiving section, that might indicate copying;
- there are striking differences between the presentation of the lead-up to the return of Jesus, with 1 Thessalonians presenting it as occurring without warning and 2 Thessalonians describing some of the events that will precede it.

No one of these pieces of evidence in and of itself can (nor should) prove convincing concerning the authenticity of the letter (cf. Trilling 1972: 45). Taken together, however, they provide circumstantial evidence for or against the letter having been composed by the same group that wrote 1 Thessalonians: Paul, Silvanus and Timothy. That scholars continue to debate this issue demonstrates that it is far from conclusive. As a result, 2 Thessalonians is classified as 'deutero-Pauline' (i.e. 'secondarily' Pauline) rather than pseudo-Pauline (i.e. falsely attributed to Paul). To my mind there is enough evidence to indicate that 2 Thessalonians is not authentic, and was written by person or persons unknown a generation or two after Paul's death, but genuinely felt that what they were writing is in keeping with the spirit of Paul and his companions. That said, it is not an ironclad conviction, and I remain open to having it overturned on appeal! For now, however, we will proceed with our narrative on the assumption that 2 Thessalonians was written to the Christ group in the city who were facing somewhat changed circumstances in a later generation.

Facing Adversity (2 Thess. 1.3-12 and 2.13–3.5)

The writers of 2 Thessalonians mention that Christ group members are undergoing 'persecutions and afflictions' (1.4). In the earlier letter the writers mentioned 'affliction' a couple of times (1 Thess. 1.6; 3.3, 7; cf. 3.4, translated as 'persecutions' in the NRSV). In 2 Thessalonians, however, the writers seem to be aware of an intensification of the problem and thus include 'persecution'. The Greek word rendered 'persecutions' (*diōgmoi*) makes it much clearer that this is not simply a matter of social pressure and anguish, but also involves some physical violence. What is not clear, however, is the exact nature of this persecution, nor the perpetrators behind it. Most often, the civic authorities are blamed. For example, some commentators argue that when the members of the Christ group rejected traditional religious practices, they withdrew from participating in civic cults and thus drew attention to themselves (Barclay 1993; de Vos 1999; Tellbe 2001).

As handworkers they would be expected to participate in rituals that were thought to bring protection to the city, and thus the groups received the unwelcome attention of the local authorities that were attempting to bring them back into line.

Other commentators suggest that the persecution originated at a higher level with the Roman imperial authorities in Thessalonike, who were reacting to anti-imperial rhetoric that the Christ group members learned from the Paul party and continued to use, particularly in speaking of an emissary from the heavens making an imperial arrival in the city (*parousia*) in order to inaugurate 'peace and security', thus challenging the dominance of Rome (Koester 1997; Smith 2004). Oakes (2005) surveys a number of theories that focus on persecution at the hands of imperial authorities but rejects all of them, suggesting that the letter writers are not advocating withdrawing from imperial cult *per se* but creating an alternative universe in which Jesus is at the centre.

Still other commentators move away from positing political authorities of any sort behind the persecutions, suggesting that it was rooted in conflict with local Jews in the city, as narrated in Acts 17.1-9 (Taylor 2002) and affirmed in 1 Thess. 2.13-16. When the Paul party advocated non-compliance with Torah, it created tensions between the believing Jews and Gentiles and non-believing Jews in the city, the latter of whom mounted a campaign of resistance (Still 1999) and even incited non-Jews to join into the fray (Taylor 2002). Tellbe (2001) agrees that the non-believing Jews were the troublemakers, but suggests rather that they invoked general critiques against itinerant philosophers and false prophets of the sort we noted in Chapter 3. All of these scenarios rely heavily on assuming the accuracy of the account of the Paul party's time in Thessalonike depicted in Acts 17, which we have already noted is somewhat problematic. In addition, it is not at all clear that there was any significant population of Jews in Thessalonike at this time, since there is no evidence for them in the literary or archaeological record, outside of the Book of Acts (see Ascough 2003: 191-212).

The scholarly debate continues, but whatever the cause of the persecutions and afflictions, in the face of this ongoing 'suffering' (2 Thess. 1.5), the writers note that the adherents to Christ are remaining steadfast and their faith is growing, to the point where the writers are able to boast about them (1.4). Although it is a test of their faith, they note that it will only strengthen them, and in the end justice will be served, for God will 'repay with affliction those who afflict you, and to give relief to the afflicted as well as to us' (1.6-7). The writers return to this theme in the second thanksgiving section, where they affirm the Christ group members, noting that God has called them and thus they must 'stand firm and hold fast to the traditions that you were taught by us, either by word of mouth or by our letter' (2.15). As God remains faithful to the Thessalonians, so must they remain faithful to the commands and traditions they received from the Paul party, even while suffering persecution and affliction. This is, the writers assure them, indeed what they are already doing and will go on doing (3.4).

Disorderly Banquets (2 Thess. 3.6-15)

In the concluding section of the letter, which is where one finds *paraenetic* material, that is, material that directly addresses moral attitudes and ethical behaviours, the writers give direction concerning community disruptions. In so doing, they address those who are charged with maintaining order within the group, but seemingly with the expectation that the perpetrators will receive the message at the time of the letter's reading within the gathering of the Christ group.

> We command you…to keep away from believers who are living in idleness and not according to the tradition that they received from us… For we hear that some of you are living in idleness, mere busybodies, not doing any work. Now such persons we command…to do their work quietly and to earn their own living (2 Thess. 3.6, 13).

In the NRSV translation quoted above these troublemakers are identified as 'believers who are living in idleness' (3.6). This is one possible translation of the Greek phrase *ataktōs peripatountos* that the writers employ. The second word quite literally can be rendered 'those walking about' with the word *ataktōs* indicating some type of negative behaviour such as laziness, idleness, disorderliness and disruptiveness.

'Laziness' is perhaps the most common translation and interpretation. Certainly, it fits the wider context, where the writers of 2 Thessalonians remind the group that while they were present among them they 'were not idle', they paid for their meals, and they 'worked night and day' with 'toil and labour' in order not to be a burden (3.7-8). They go on to advise that these 'idlers' should earn their keep. In this sense, the negative action is quite passive. Some believers have ceased working to earn their living and are relying on the good will and benefaction of other members in the community in order to get their meals. One possible explanation for this decision to cease working is the impending apocalypse—the end of the world—to be brought about by Jesus' coming (so Jewett 1986: 104-105; Bruce 1982: 209). Menken (1992) suggests that some members of the Christ group even thought it had already taken place (as per the rumour addressed earlier in the letter and discussed above) and as a result thought of this present life as a return to the paradise described in the early chapters of Genesis. In his view, the letter writers are attempting to show that there is still some distance between their experience of the present and the future restoration of paradise.

If 'laziness' reflects passive inactivity, another possible translation gives the text a much more active thrust, interpreting the Greek phrase as indicating that some members are 'walking about disruptively'. Certainly this fits with the writers' concern that some of these people are acting as 'busybodies' (3.11). Jewett (1986: 176-78) suggests that these people not only have given up working in the face of the return or Jesus but also are actively spreading false rumours about the event among their fellow believers.

Other commentators argue that the problem is actually not rooted in eschatological expectation or speculation. Rather, some members of the Christ group, particularly those who are impoverished day labourers, are taking advantage of benefaction of more wealthy members (Russell 1988; Winter 1989). As we noted in Chapter 4, patronage was a ubiquitous part of associative life in the Greco-Roman context, and thus it would be no surprise that some saw it as a means to avoid paying an equal share for the maintenance of the group. That said, examples of outright cessation of work among association members on the basis of expectations of the largess of others are difficult to find. On the other hand, we have plenty of evidence that associations experienced and disciplined disruptive members, since many of them recorded their legislation for doing so on inscriptions. My own understanding of this text is grounded in such data (the following is a summary of Ascough 2010).

The linchpin for interpreting this text occurs in the injunction that is to be enacted against the troublemakers: 'anyone unwilling to work should not eat', a command that the letter writers note was given to the Thessalonians while the Paul party was in the city at the group's very founding (3.10). As a whole, the text presents us with the following picture: there is a sub-group among the adherents of Christ in Thessalonike who refuse to work and instead are acting as 'busybodies'. This is particularly striking in the context of a group that is, at its core, formed from a workers' association as we argued in Chapter 1. Working with their hands is at the core of what has brought the group together even before they made their collective allegiance to God through Christ. By refusing to work with their hands, these members are unsettling the very foundation of the group.

In contrast, the rest of the group is 'doing and will go on doing' the things that the Paul party command, including the 'work to eat' ruling. In the earlier letter we noted that the writers advocated they continue working with their hands (1 Thess. 4.11) in much the same way Paul and his companions did while among them (1 Thess. 2.9). In this later letter, those who have continued their daily labour are told to shun the troublemakers with a very clear command: 'keep away from them' (2 Thess. 3.6, cf. 3.14). Yet these troublemakers are not to be viewed as non-members of the group, for the writers first refer to them as 'believers' (3.6) and end by urging the faithful not to 'regard them as enemies, but warn them as believers' (3.15).

While the writers of 2 Thessalonians decry those who are acting contrary to the group norms and not pulling their weight (either through laziness or disruptiveness, or both), their solution to fixing this problem must be enforceable. It is difficult to imagine that in commanding, 'let them not eat', they are advocating death by starvation. The faithful cannot control whether or not the disruptive members eat elsewhere. Thus, the command must focus on what takes place internally to the group, where it is possible to enforce the regulation. This regulation is best understood as a ban from communal meals.

Literary texts mentioning associations often comment on their meal practices, largely in noting the uncivilized behaviours that resulted from the eating and drinking. For example, the Jewish philosopher Philo was clearly not impressed with the banquet practices of associations in second-century Alexandria, Egypt, particularly since a local opponent of the Judeans in the city had used the association to his own advantage:

> There are associations in the city with a large membership whose fellowship [*koinōnia*] is founded on no good principle. Instead, they are united by strong wine, drunkenness, drinking, and the outcome of those indulgencies: wanton violence. Their meetings are called 'synods' and 'dining-couches' by the locals. In all these societies, or the majority of them, Isidorus held the highest place and was called leader of the banquet, chief of the dining-couch, and disturber of the city. Then, whenever he wanted to cause some damage, at his signal they all came together in a body, and they did and said whatever they were told (*AGRW* L10).

Even among inscriptions set up by the association, meals are often a concern, if not the primary concern, of regulations around membership and behavior—what to eat, when, where, by whom, along with issues of who supplies the funds and who gets the bigger portion of the food (on association meals, see Ascough 2012). A typical example can be seen in an inscription of the Iobacchoi at Athens (*AGRW* 7, c. 178 CE), which proscribes expulsion for rule breakers:

> If one of those who enters does not pay the entrance fee to the priest or the vice-priest, he shall be expelled from the banquet until he pays and he shall pay in whatever way the priest orders… The one who made the disturbance shall leave the banquet hall. If he refuses, those who have been appointed by the priests as 'horses' [i.e. bouncers] shall take him outside of the door.

Other associations had similar regulations against bad behaviour, both at general meetings and especially at banquets.

The legislation invoked in 2 Thess. 3.6-15 stipulates that a person who chooses not to integrate into the group shall not be welcome at the meals, both regular banquets and perhaps a ritualized meal such as the 'Lord's Supper', if this takes place at Thessalonike in the way it did in Corinth

(1 Cor. 11.23-26). The writers are commanding that disruptive members are placed outside the group's social boundaries until they have 'learned their lesson' as demonstrated through ceasing their disruptive behaviour and carrying their share of the workload, after which they can be reintegrated into the group.

Clearly there is a problem within the Thessalonian Christ group to which the writers of 2 Thessalonians offer a solution that emphasizes equal and reciprocal relationships. The Thessalonians are to remain faithful to one another in the same way that God has been faithful to them and they to God. Mutual support rather than selfish pursuits will strengthen the community (Roetzel 1986; Witmer 2006). The writers assure the Christ group members that by reducing their anxiety concerning Jesus' coming (2.1-12), remaining faithful in the face of external opposition (1.3-12, 2.13–3.5), and working hard and preserving decorum during group meetings and meals (3.6-15), they will come to experience God's peace 'at all times in all ways' (3.16). Although not composed by the same writers of 1 Thessalonians, the letter gives us a glimpse into developments in the Christ group at Thessalonike at a later time, perhaps towards the end of the first century, and thus how they needed to adapt and adjusting their interactions for new circumstances.

Our story of the early Christ group is drawing to a close. From that hot, dusty day in the mid-first century when Paul, Silvanus, Timothy, and perhaps a few others entered Thessalonike we have been able to construct a bit of the group's history. Paul and his companions settled into a workshop where they were able to convince an extant occupational group to switch their allegiance to a new patron deity—the God of Jesus Christ. Bolstered by the message of escape from a 'coming wrath', they proclaimed this new allegiance to friends, families, customers, suppliers and an assortment of travellers they happened to encounter. Although most were not likely convinced that this new eastern God was worthy of such trust, they were nevertheless intrigued enough to gossip about the Thessalonian group's commitment, and thus the 'word about the Lord' spread south-eastward at least as far as Athens and Corinth, even before the Paul party arrived in these other locales.

Having left somewhat suddenly, the Paul party sent Timothy back to Thessalonike to see how the community was faring. When he returned, Timothy brought news of their continued faithfulness, although they were somewhat put out that Paul and the others departed so quickly, and were feeling a bit like they might have been duped by charlatans. In addition, they had some very specific questions concerning community relations, particularly the status of those who had already died and perhaps missed out on the coming of Jesus. Paul, Silvanus and Timothy collectively composed a letter not only answering these questions, but also reassuring the Christ group members of the Paul party's deep and abiding care for them. This letter would later come to be known as '1 Thessalonians'.

We temporarily lose sight of the Thessalonian Christ group, but pick up the story again in the next generation of believers, perhaps around the 80s or 90s of the first century. It seems there was still an active group of Christ devotees in the city, but they had become somewhat distraught over rumours that Jesus had already appeared and somehow they missed out on the event. Knowing that they needed reassurance, a well-meaning leader, either within the group or in another Pauline community, composed a letter to them, using the names of Paul, Silvanus and Timothy as authors in order to give legitimacy and authority to the content. This was not an attempt to deceive the Thessalonian Christ group members, for it was a common enough practice in antiquity. When the group encountered the letter—we can perhaps imagine that leaders 'discovered' it in the group archives— they learned that their own fears had already been addressed in the previous generation. This letter also tackled an important practical issue, that of believing members who had disengaged from the group occupation and were creating disturbances at meals. The anonymous letter writer(s) recommended disciplinary action. This letter would later come to be known as '2 Thessalonians'.

At this point, we encounter a fork in our historical narrative. One path traces the history of the Thessalonian Christ group itself, while the other path follows the history of the two letters within the wider Christian community. We will begin with the community itself, although not much at all is known from the second and third centuries, except that one or more Christ groups maintained a presence in Thessalonike. According to Origen (184/185–253/254 CE) in his *Commentary on Romans*, the first bishop of Thessalonike was Gaius, Paul's host in Corinth (Rom. 16.23; cf. 1 Cor. 1.14), although this seems unlikely, and Origen has probably blended the Corinthian Gaius with a Macedonian of the same name mentioned as a travelling companion of Paul in Acts 19.29. In his list of the 70 apostles, Hippolytus of Rome (170–235 CE) names Silvanus as the first Thessalonian bishop (*On the End of the World* 49), a slightly more likely choice given Silvanus' role in the founding of the Thessalonian Christ group and as one of the co-writers of the letter. Yet, as is the case with many of the attributions of 'first bishop' status to first generation Christ followers named in the New Testament, this is probably spurious. It is not until we approach the fourth century that more concrete evidence for the Christian activity in Thessalonike becomes available.

Towards the end of the third century a number of Christians were put to death for their faith during a period of Christian maltreatment at the directive of the emperor Diocletian towards the end of his reign (302–305) and continued by his successor Galerius (305–311). In Thessalonike this included three sisters—Agape, Chionia and Irene—who died in 304 at the hands of the Macedonian governor. It was during this time that there arose a man who is perhaps the most famous among the Thessalonian Christians: Demetrios, whose life and death earned him the status of patron saint of the city (see Skedros 1999). Demetrios was born to Christian parents around 270 CE and was a full Roman citizen. Because of his faith, he ran afoul of the local authorities, and during a visit of the emperor Galarius to Thessalonike sometime between 304 and 308 CE, Demetrios was run through with spears. A church was later built on the Roman bath complex that was the site of his death, and Demetrios was recognized as a martyr and a hero, becoming venerated in the mid-seventh century as a saint and the divine patron and protector of Thessalonike. The church building continued to be developed, and the basilica of Hagios Demetrios remains standing today a few blocks north of the ancient agora, in the centre of the city.

In an ironic twist, the Rotunda built by Galarius, perhaps as his mausoleum, was converted into a church, perhaps by the end of the fourth century, indicating the continued flourishing of the Thessalonian Christian groups in the post-Galarian period. In the two subsequent centuries other monuments built by Galarius were converted into churches, alongside the construction of new church buildings. We can thus see evidence of Christianity flourishing in Thessalonike (see the essays in Breytenbach and Behrmann 2007; cf. Adam-Veleni 2003: 171-72). This parallels the developments across the entire Roman Empire during the Byzantine period, and in the post-Constantine period successive bishops of Thessalonike participated in important church councils.

After the division of the church 'universal' into the eastern and western branches (1054 CE), ecclesial leaders in Thessalonike fell under the authority of the Patriarch of Constantinople, and at times the city itself was granted 'co-reigning' status. During the Ottoman period (1430–1912) the churches fell into decline, with many of them being converted into mosques. Since independence in 1912, the Greek Orthodox Church has revived and many church buildings have been restored in the modern metropolis of Thessaloniki.

We noted earlier the divergent paths towards the end of the first century, the historical path that we have just outlined and that of the letters themselves, to which we now briefly turn our attention. As Friesen (2010) demonstrates, the unknown writer's use of the names of Paul, Silvanus and Timothy in 2 Thessalonians marks an early shift from letters as a means of communication to letters as repositories of authoritative and divinely sanctioned truths, that is, a step towards the canonization process. By the second century, both of the letters to the Thessalonians were accepted as having relevance and authority in the Christian community across the Roman Empire. As such, they receive occasional reference and quotation in the writings of the second-century Christian intelligentsia, who used the texts to support their own developing theologies.

Both letters are included in the various canonical lists that were produced during this time, both the truncated version of the heterodox Marcion (mid-second century CE) and the more widely accepted 'Muratorian canon' (c. 200 CE). Although they are listed in their chronological order, and thus deemed 'first' and 'second' Thessalonians, this is a result of their relative length rather than an attention to history. All of the Pauline letters that eventually were accepted into the Christian canon appear according to their length, with Romans being the longest letter addressed to an entire Christ group and 2 Thessalonians being the shortest. There follows four more letters, again arranged according to size, and collected together because they are addressed to individuals rather than entire communities (1 and 2 Timothy, Titus, Philemon). When the canonical list of New Testament books was finalized at the Councils of Carthage in 397 and 419 CE, both 1 and 2 Thessalonians made the cut with little opposition.

Since that time, they have, like all biblical books, been subject to continued interpretive use (and abuse) in the church. The earliest commentaries on the two letters were produced in the fourth and fifth centuries by the 'Antiochene' school of theology that had as their focus a concern with the historical meaning of the texts. As Wanamaker (2005: 148-49) points out, the suggestion in 1 Thessalonians that the writers would be alive at the coming of Jesus (4.15) created a bit of a thorny problem because they were by all accounts not correct. As a result, the Antiochene interpreters simply deny that this verse is self-referential, thus avoiding the implications that the writers were wrong. It is an interpretive move that has continued throughout Christian history.

This is only one of many different exegetical moves undertaken throughout the history of interpretation of the eschatological passages in 1 and 2 Thessalonians (4.13–5.11 and 2.1-12, respectively). These texts have drawn more attention than any other passages in the two letters. In the Middle Ages they tended to be allegorized, that is, given symbolic meaning and thus avoiding issues of the timing and nature of events surrounding the coming of Jesus. In the post-Reformation period, the Protestant tradition in particular returned to literal and historical exegesis (Wanamaker 2005: 149), and thus set the stage for using both letters in apocalyptic speculation, a trend that has not only continued into our own day but has also flourished.

Despite the declaration in 1 Thessalonians that the timing of Jesus' return cannot be known (5.2-3; cf. Mk 13.32, 1 Pet. 3.10), many commentators from the patristic period through to today have treated 2 Thess. 2.1-12 as prophecy and connected the images therein to events in their own time and place (Wanamaker 2005: 155-56). The 'man of lawlessness' (2 Thess. 2.3-4) was merged with the antichrist figure referenced in the letters of John (1 Jn 2.18, 22; 4.3; 2 Jn 7), and then further merged with one of the beasts in the Book of Revelation, namely, the one whose name is represented numerically as '666' (Rev. 13.11-18). Although separate figures described by different authors for different audiences at different times, this theological merger has produced no end of speculation as to who is the person (or thing) that embodies the ultimate evil that will mark the final epoch of human history into which God will send God's son to punish the evil and reward the faithful.

A second eschatological development that has deep cultural impact in the modern period is the notion of the 'rapture', a term coined by John Nelson Darby in the mid-nineteenth century. It is based in large part on the description of living believers being 'caught up' (1 Thess. 4.16-17). In

Darby's schema (and others that follow him, particularly in Western conservative evangelical Christianity), the rapture is an event that is distinct from the coming of Jesus. The gathering of Christians 'in the air' at the time of the rapture marks a key point in the establishing of God's millennial kingdom. We cannot here go into the entire history of apocalyptic thought, and others have done so well enough (e.g. Kyle 1998; Court 2008). Suffice it to say that both 1 Thessalonians and, especially, 2 Thessalonians, loom large in discussions of the end of the world as we know it, although often with too little attention to either the literary or social context in which the letters were first written.

At this point, we must draw our narrative to a conclusion. I hope you will agree that constructing the history of the Thessalonian Christian community through an exploration of the two letters addressed to that community has proved interesting. From these two very short letters we learn not only about the formation and subsequent organization of the Christ group in the city, we can also learn about what issues troubled them, and how their founders—particularly Paul, Silvanus and Timothy—provided advice and affirmation for their behaviour and their belief. As an introductory text, this book has only begun to scratch the surface. We have highlighted places where there is general agreement, and other places, many of them, where interpretations are in conflict. Much work remains to be done. This book has attempted to lay the groundwork for the reader to take the next steps of historical reconstruction and exegetical interpretation. And to the next generation of biblical scholars might I be so bold to speak on behalf of all of us who have gone before and say, by paraphrasing 1 Thess. 4.1, that as you have learned from us, do so 'more and more'. We look forward to the new insights that will arise and the challenges that will be mounted as we work together to understand the Christ group at Thessalonike and the letters they received from Paul and his companions.

BIBLIOGRAPHY

Many scholarly commentaries, books, and articles have been published on 1 and 2 Thessalonians. Here we can only give a brief sense of some of the major English language commentaries, along with a listing of the works that are cited in the foregoing text. For an extensive annotated bibliography up to 1998 readers should consult Weima and Porter 1998. This is complemented and supplemented with my own contribution of about 150 entries on 'Thessalonians' in *Oxford Bibliographies Online* (Ascough 2011b).

Major English Language Commentaries

Beale, G.K., *1–2 Thessalonians* (IVP New Testament Commentary Series; Downers Grove, IL: InterVarsity, 2003).

> The predominant aim of this commentary is to move from exposition to sermons and Bible studies. It has a decidedly evangelical perspective and uses the New International Version.

Best, Ernest, *The First and Second Epistles to the Thessalonians* (BNTC; London: A. & C. Black, 1972 [repr. Peabody, MA: Hendrickson, 1986]).

> Although dated, Best's commentary is one of the few English language critical commentaries to appear between Frame 1912 and the late 1990s. His comments are based on his own translation of the Greek text and give good insight into the lexical nuances of Greek words, with some dipping into Hebrew antecedents (both of which are often not translated).

Bruce, F.F., *1 & 2 Thessalonians* (WBC, 45; Waco, TX: Word, 1982).

> Each section begins with a literal translation of the Greek text, followed by comments on the form, structure and setting. The clause-by-clause observations are based on the Greek text, so this commentary will be of most use to those who have studied Greek for a year or more. His comments are generally conservative from the evangelical framework. He considers both letters to have been written by Paul.

Fee, Gordon D., *The First and Second Letters to the Thessalonians* (NICNT; Grand Rapids: Eerdmans, 2009).

> Fee bases his verse-by-verse exegetical comments on the English text and treats both letters as authentic. He is conversant with biblical scholarship but makes it accessible for ministers and for students in the evangelical tradition.

Frame, James E., *The Epistles of St. Paul to the Thessalonians* (ICC; Edinburgh: T. & T. Clark, 1912).

> Although this commentary is over 100 years old, many of Frame's observations on the words used in each verse are still interesting and help situate the texts in their linguistic as well as their social contexts. References to Greek will limit this commentary's appeal to those who know the original language of the letters.

Furnish, Victor Paul, *1 Thessalonians. 2 Thessalonians* (ANTC; Nashville: Abingdon
    Press, 2007).
    Provides some basic exegetical insights for students, seminarians, and pastors.
    Furnish treats 1 Thessalonians as the earliest of Paul's letters, but 2 Thessalonians
    as written after Paul's death and thus as providing insight into the interpretation of
    Paul in the late first century.
Gaventa, Beverly Roberts, *First and Second Thessalonians* (Interpretation; Louisville,
    KY: John Knox Press, 1998).
    Gaventa provides a readable commentary on each section of the text, followed by
    reflections on how the text could be applied in the modern church. It will primarily
    appeal to those involved in preaching and teaching in church contexts.
Gorday, Peter (ed.), *Ancient Christian Commentary on Scripture. New Testament IX.
    Colossians, 1–2 Thessalonians, 1–2 Timothy, Titus, Philemon* (Downers Grove,
    IL: InterVarsity Press, 2000).
    Lengthy, extended commentaries are not just a product of modern biblical scholar-
    ship. Christian teachers and preachers throughout the ages have made interpretive
    notes on New Testament texts. In this volume, Gorday gathers such comments on
    1 and 2 Thessalonians from writers from the first through eighth centuries.
Green, Gene L., *The Letters to the Thessalonians* (Pillar New Testament Commentary;
    Grand Rapids: Eerdmans, 2002).
    Green uses a variety of archaeological and literary material to provide the setting
    of Thessalonike and thus the readers of both letters, which he treats as written by
    Paul in their current order. His verse-by-verse exegesis aims to show how the text
    would have impacted the original readers. The commentary is written primarily for
    pastors and Bible teachers, and thus includes comments on how the text informs
    the modern church.
Malherbe, Abraham J., *The Letters to the Thessalonians: A New Translation with Intro-
    duction and Commentary* (AB, 32B; New York: Doubleday, 2000).
    Malherbe spent much of his career as a professor at Yale working on various facets
    of 1 and 2 Thessalonians. This commentary encapsulates much of this work as
    he provides detailed observations on the linguistic and social worlds of the texts.
    His work can best be described as historical-critical and since its publication has
    served scholars well as a foundation for their own research. It can be quite techni-
    cal and thus will have less appeal to the general reader.
Morris, Leon, *The First and Second Epistles to the Thessalonians* (NICNT; Grand
    Rapids: Eerdmans, rev. edn, 1991).
    Originally published in 1959, the revised edition provides solid, if conservative,
    exegetical observations based on the New International Version translation. It is
    more theological than historical in its approach and treats both letters as authentic.
    It has been replaced in the series by Fee 2009.
Richard, Earl J., *First and Second Thessalonians* (SP, 11; Collegeville, MN: Liturgical
    Press, 1995).
    Richard pays particular attention to the formal features of both letters, although
    he also provides comments on the texts and themes of each. Richard argues that
    1 Thessalonians is composed of two letters, while 2 Thessalonians comes from a
    later time. Although the comments can have a Catholic slant, the commentary is
    broad enough to appeal to a wider audience.
Smith, Abraham, 'The First Letter to the Thessalonians: Introduction, Commentary, and
    Reflections' and 'The Second Letter to the Thessalonians: Introduction, Commen-

tary, and Reflections', in *The New Interpreter's Bible. A Commentary in Twelve Volumes, Vol. XI, 2 Corinthians, Galatians, Ephesians, Philippians, Colossians, 1 and 2 Thessalonians, 1 and 2 Timothy, Titus, Philemon* (ed. Harriett Jane Olson; Nashville: Abingdon Press, 2000), pp. 671-737 and 739-72.

Linguistic, text-critical, historical-critical, literary, social-scientific and theological methods provide a rich diversity of observations using the NRSV and NIV translations. Concluding reflections link the texts to modern Christian faith and practice.

Wanamaker, Charles A., *The Epistles to the Thessalonians: A Commentary on the Greek Text* (NIGTC; Grand Rapids: Eerdmans, 1990).

Wannamaker provides the best available application of Aristotelian rhetorical categories to both letters, alongside astute linguistic insights. The commentary is, however, quite technical and thus best suited for scholars and upper-level students. He creatively argues that although both letters are written by Paul, the shorter letter (2 Thessalonians) was sent before the longer.

Witherington III, Ben, *1 and 2 Thessalonians: A Socio-Rhetorical Commentary* (Grand Rapids: Eerdmans, 2006).

Although the commentary does not cohere with a technical understanding of 'socio-rhetorical', it does pay due attention to the social world of Paul and the Thessalonians and it does attempt to understand the type of rhetorical moves made in the texts. Witherington views both letters coming from Paul, who seeks to challenge and subvert Roman imperialism in his language and images. It is perhaps most useful for preachers in the evangelical tradition.

Works Cited

Adam-Veleni, Polyxeni

2003   'Thessaloniki: History and Town Planning', in *Roman Thessaloniki* (ed. D.V. Grammenos; Thessaloniki Archaeological Museum Publications, 1; Thessalonike: Thessaloniki Archaeological Museum): 121-76.

Ascough, Richard S.

2000   'The Thessalonian Christian Community as a Professional Voluntary Association', *JBL* 119: 311-28.

2003   *Paul's Macedonian Associations: The Social Context of Philippians and 1 Thessalonians* (WUNT, II/161; Tübingen: Mohr Siebeck).

2004   'A Question of Death: Paul's Community Building Language in 1 Thessalonians 4:13-18', *JBL* 123: 509-30.

2009a   *Lydia: Paul's Cosmopolitan Hostess* (Paul's Social Network: Brothers and Sisters in Faith; Collegeville, MN: Liturgical Press).

2009b   'Thessalonians, First Letter to', in Sakenfeld 2009: 569-74.

2009c   'Thessalonians, Second Letter to', in Sakenfeld 2009: 574-79.

2010   'Of Memories and Meals: Greco-Roman Associations and the Early Jesus-group at Thessalonikē', in Nasrallah, Bakirtzis and Friesen 2010: 49-72.

2011a   'Paul's "Apocalypticism" and the Jesus-Associations at Thessalonica and Corinth', in *Redescribing Paul and the Corinthians* (ed. Ron Cameron and Merrill P. Miller; ECL, 5; Atlanta: Scholars Press): 151-86.

2011b   'Thessalonians', in *Oxford Bibliographies Online: Biblical Studies* (ed. Christopher Matthews; Oxford: Oxford University Press, online at http://aboutobo.com/biblical-studies).

2012   'Social and Political Characteristics of Greco-Roman Association Meals', in *Meals in the Early Christian World: Social Formation, Experimentation, and*

Conflict at the Table (ed. Dennis E. Smith and Hal Taussig; New York: Palgrave MacMillan): 59-72.

2014   'Re-describing the Thessalonian's "Mission" in Light of Graeco-Roman Associations', *NTS* 60/1: 61-82.

Ascough, Richard S., Philip A. Harland and John S. Kloppenborg

2012   *Associations in the Greco-Roman World: A Sourcebook* (Waco, TX: Baylor University Press). Further texts and resources can be found on the accompanying website at http://philipharland.com/greco-roman-associations.

Bailey, John A.

1978/79   'Who Wrote II Thessalonians?', *NTS* 25: 131-45.

Bassler, Jouette M.

1995   '*Skeuos*: A Modest Proposal for Illuminating Paul's Use of Metaphor in 1 Thessalonians 4:4', in *The Social World of the First Christians: Essays in Honor of Wayne A. Meeks* (ed. L. Michael White and O. Larry Yarbrough; Minneapolis: Fortress Press): 53-66.

Barclay, John M.G.

1993   'Conflict at Thessalonica', *CBQ* 55: 512-30.

Beale, G.K.

2003   *1–2 Thessalonians* (IVP New Testament Commentary Series; Downers Grove, IL: InterVarsity Press).

Blumenthal, Christian

2005   'Was sagt 1 Thess 1.9b-10 über die Adressaten des 1 Thess? Literarische und historische Erwägungen', *NTS* 51: 96-105.

Bowers, Paul

1991   'Church and Mission in Paul', *JSNT* 44: 89-111.

Breytenbach, Cilliers, and Ingrid Behrmann (eds.)

2007   *Frühchristlichs Thessaloniki* (STAC, 44; Tübingen: Mohr Siebeck).

Brocke, Christoph vom

2001   *Thessaloniki, Stadt des Kassander und Gemeinde des Paulus: Eine frühe christliche Gemeinde in ihrer heidnischen Umwelt* (WUNT, II/125; Tübingen: Mohr Siebeck).

Bruce, F.F.

1982   *1 and 2 Thessalonians* (WBC, 45; Waco, TX: Word).

Burke, Trevor J.

2003   *Family Matters: A Socio-Historical Study of Kinship Metaphors in 1 Thessalonians* (JSNTSup, 247; London: T. & T. Clark International).

Chapa, Juan

1994   'Is First Thessalonians a Letter of Consolation?', *NTS* 40: 150-60.

Collins, Raymond F.

1984   *Studies on the First Letter to the Thessalonians* (BETL, 66; Leuven: Leuven University Press).

1990a   '"The Gospel of our Lord Jesus Christ" (2 Thes 1,8): A Symbolic Shift of Paradigm', in Collins 1990b: 426-40.

Collins, Raymond F. (ed.)

1990b   *The Thessalonian Correspondence* (BETL, 87; Leuven: Leuven University Press).

Coulot, Claude

2006   'Paul à Thessalonique (1Th 2.1-12)', *NTS* 52: 377-93.

Court, John M.
  2008   *Approaching the Apocalypse: A Short History of Christian Millenarianism* (London and New York: I.B. Tauris).
Crüsemann, Marlene
  2010   *Die pseudepigraphen Briefe an die Gemeinde in Thessaloniki: Studien zu ihrer Abfassung und zur jüdisch-christlichen Sozialgeschichte* (BWANT, 191; Stuttgart: Kohlhammer).
Davies, Jon
  1999   *Death, Burial and Rebirth in the Religions of Antiquity* (Religion in the First Christian Centuries; London and New York: Routledge).
Dickson, John P.
  2003   *Mission-Commitment in Ancient Judaism and in the Pauline Communities: The Shape, Extent and Background of Early Christian Mission* (WUNT, II/159; Tübingen: Mohr Siebeck).
Donfried, Karl P.
  1984   'Paul and Judaism: 1 Thessalonians 2.13-16 as a Test Case', *Int* 38: 242-53.
  1985   'The Cults of Thessalonica and the Thessalonian Correspondence', *NTS* 31: 336-56.
  1993   'The Theology of 2 Thessalonians', in *The Theology of the Shorter Pauline Letters* (ed. Karl P. Donfried and I. Howard Marshall; Testament Theology; Cambridge, UK: Cambridge University Press): 81-113.
  2002   *Paul, Thessalonica, and Early Christianity* (Grand Rapids: Eerdmans).
Donfried, Karl P., and Johannes Beutler (eds.)
  2000   *The Thessalonians Debate: Methodological Discord or Methodological Synthesis?* (Grand Rapids: Eerdmans).
Edson, Charles
  1948   'Cults of Thessalonica (Macedonia III)', *HTR* 41: 153-204.
Elgvin, Torlief
  1997   '"To Master his own Vessel": 1 Thess 4.4 in Light of New Qumran Evidence', *NTS* 43: 604-19.
Fee, Gordon D.
  2009   *The First and Second Letters to the Thessalonians* (NICNT; Grand Rapids: Eerdmans).
Frame, James E.
  1912   *The Epistles of St. Paul to the Thessalonians* (ICC; Edinburgh: T. & T. Clark).
Friesen, Steven J.
  2010   'Second Thessalonians, the Ideology of Epistles, and the Construction of Authority: Our Debt to the Forger', in Nasrallah, Bakirtzis and Friesen (2010): 189-210.
Gilliard, Frank D.
  1989   'The Problem of the Antisemitic Comma between 1 Thessalonians 2.14 and 15', *NTS* 35: 481-502.
Graf, Fritz, and Sarah Iles Johnston
  2007   *Ritual Texts for the Afterlife: Orpheus and the Bacchic Gold Tablets* (London and New York: Routledge).
Green, Gene L.
  2002   *The Letters to the Thessalonians* (Pillar New Testament Commentary; Grand Rapids: Eerdmans).

Hardin, Justin K.
2006 'Decrees and Drachmas at Thessalonica: An Illegal Assembly in Jason's House (Acts 17.1-10a)', *NTS* 52: 29-49.
Harrison, James R.
2010 *Paul and the Imperial Authorities at Thessalonica and Rome: A Study in the Conflict of Ideology* (WUNT, 273; Tübingen: Mohr Siebeck).
Hock, Ronald F.
1980 *The Social Context of Paul's Ministry: Tentmaking and Apostleship* (Philadelphia: Fortress Press).
Holland, Glenn Stanfield
1988 *The Tradition that You Received from Us: 2 Thessalonians in the Pauline Tradition* (HUT, 24; Tübingen: Mohr Siebeck).
1990 '"A Letter Supposedly from Us": A Contribution to the Discussion about the Authorship of 2 Thessalonians', in Collins 1990b: 394-402.
Holtz, Traugott
1990 'The Judgment on the Jews and the Salvation of All Israel. 1 Thes 2,15-16 and Rom 11,25-26', in Collins 1990b: 284-94.
Hoppe, Rudolf
1997 'Der erste Thessalonicherbrief und die antike Rhetorik', *BZ* 41: 229-37.
Hughes, Frank Witt
1989 *Early Christian Rhetoric and 2 Thessalonians* (JSNTSup, 30; Sheffield: JSOT Press).
1990 'The Rhetoric of 1 Thessalonians', in Collins 1990b: 94-116.
Hurd, John C.
1998 *The Earlier Letters of Paul—and Other Studies* (Studies in the Religion and History of Early Christianity, 8; New York: Peter Lang).
Jewett, Robert
1986 *The Thessalonian Correspondence: Pauline Rhetoric and Millenarian Piety* (Philadelphia: Fortress Press).
1993 'Tenement Churches and Communal Meals in the Early Church: The Implications of a Form-Critical Analysis of 2 Thessalonians 3:10', *BibRes* 38: 23-43.
Kloppenborg, John S.
1993 'ΦΙΛΑΔΕΛΦΙΑ, ΘΕΟΔΙΔΑΚΤΟΣ and the Dioscuri: Rhetorical Engagement in 1 Thessalonians 4:9-12', *NTS* 39: 265-89.
Kloppenborg, John S., and Richard S. Ascough
2011 *Greco-Roman Associations: Texts, Translations, and Commentary*. I. *Attica, Central Greece, Macedonia, Thrace* (BZNW, 181; Berlin and New York: W. de Gruyter).
Koester, Helmut
1997 'Imperial Ideology and Paul's Eschatology in 1 Thessalonians', in *Paul and Empire: Religion and Power in Roman Imperial Society* (ed. Richard A. Horsley; Harrisburg, PA: Trinity Press International): 158-66.
2010 'Egyptian Religion in Thessalonikē: Regulation for the Cult', in Nasrallah, Bakirtzis and Friesen (2010): 133-50.
Kyle, Richard
1998 *The Last Days Are Here Again: A History of the End Times* (Grand Rapids: Baker).

Lamp, Jeffrey S.
  2003   'Is Paul Anti-Jewish? Testament of Levi 6 in the Interpretation of 1 Thessalonians 2:13-16', *CBQ* 65: 408-27.
Laub, Franz
  1976   'Paulus als Gemeindegründer (1 Thess)', in *Kirche im Werden: Studien zum Thema Amt und Gemeinde im Neuen Testament* (ed. Josef Hainz; Munich: Schöningh): 17-38.
Luckensmeyer, David
  2009   *The Eschatology of First Thessalonians* (NTOA, 71; Göttingen:: Vandenhoeck & Ruprecht).
Lührmann, Dieter
  1990   'The Beginnings of the Church at Thessalonica', in *Greeks, Romans, and Christians: Essays in Honor of Abraham J. Malherbe* (ed. David L. Balch, Wayne A. Meeks and Everett Ferguson; Minneapolis: Fortress Press): 237-49.
Malherbe, Abraham J.
  1970   '"Gentile as a Nurse": The Cynic Background to 1 Thessalonians 2', *NovT* 12: 203-17.
  1987   *Paul and the Thessalonians: The Philosophic Tradition of Pastoral Care* (Philadelphia: Fortress Press).
  1989   *Paul and the Popular Philosophers* (Minneapolis: Fortress Press).
  1990   'Did the Thessalonians Write to Paul?', in *The Conversation Continues: Studies in Paul and John in Honor of J. Louis Martyn* (ed. Robert Fortna and Beverly Gaventa; Nashville: Abingdon Press): 246-57.
  1992   'Hellenistic Moralists and the New Testament', *ANRW* II 26/3: 267-333.
  2000   *The Letters to the Thessalonians: A New Translation with Introduction and Commentary* (AB, 32B; New York: Doubleday).
Malina, Bruce J.
  2003   'Understanding New Testament Persons', in *The Social Sciences and New Testament Interpretation* (ed. Richard L. Rohrbaugh; Peabody, MA: Hendrickson): 41-61.
McGehee, Michael
  1989   'A Rejoinder to Two Recent Studies Dealing with 1 Thessalonians 4:4', *CBQ* 51: 82-89.
Menken, Maarten J.J.
  1992   'Paradise Regained or Still Lost: Eschatology and Disorderly Behaviour in 2 Thessalonians', *NTS* 38: 271-89.
  1994   *2 Thessalonians* (London and New York: Routledge).
Morris, Leon
  1991   *The First and Second Epistles to the Thessalonians* (NICNT; Grand Rapids: Eerdmans, rev. edn).
Nasrallah, Laura, Charalambos Bakirtzis and Steven J. Friesen (eds.)
  2010   *From Roman to Early Christian Thessalonikē: Studies in Religion and Archaeology* (HTS, 64; Cambridge, MA, and London: Harvard University Press).
Nicholl, Colin R.
  2004   *From Hope to Despair in Thessalonica: Situating 1 and 2 Thessalonians* (SNTSMS, 126; Cambridge: Cambridge University Press).
Oakes, Peter
  2005   'Re-mapping the Universe: Paul and the Emperor in 1 Thessalonians and Philippians', *JSNT* 27: 301-22.

Pahl, Michael W.

2009 *Discerning the 'Word of the Lord': The 'Word of the Lord' in 1 Thessalonians 4:15* (LNTS, 389; New York and London: T. & T. Clark).

Pearson, Birger A.

1971 '1 Thessalonians 2:13-16: A Deutero-Pauline Interpolation', *HTR* 64: 79-94.

Reinmuth, Eckart

1998 'Der erste Brief an die Thessalonicher', in *Die Briefe an die Philipper, Thessalonicher und an Philemon* (ed. Walter Nikolaus, Eckart Reinmuth and Peter Lampe; Das Neue Testament Deutsch, 8/2. Göttingen: Vandenhoeck & Ruprecht): 157-202.

Richard, Earl J.

1995 *First and Second Thessalonians* (SP, 11; Collegeville, MN: Liturgical Press).

Richards, E. Randolph

2005 *Paul and First Century Letter Writing: Secretaries, Composition and Collection* (Grand Rapids: InterVarsity Press).

Rigaux, Béda

1956 *Saint Paul: Les Épitres aux Thessaloniciens* (ÉBib; Paris: Gabalda).

Robbins, Vernon K.

2009 *The Invention of Christian Discourse. I. Rhetoric of Religious Antiquity* (Blandford Forum: Deo).

Roetzel, Calvin J.

1986 '*Theodidaktoi* and Handwork in Philo and I Thessalonians', in *Apôtre Paul: Personnalité, style et conception du ministère* (ed. Albert Vanhoye; BETL, 73; Leuven, Belgium: Peeters): 324-31.

1998 *The Letters of Paul: Conversations in Context* (Louisville, KY: Westminster/John Knox Press, 4th edn).

Russell, Ronald

1988 'The Idle in 2 Thess 3.6-12: An Eschatological or a Social Problem?', *NTS* 34: 105-19.

Sakenfeld, Katherine Doob (ed.)

2009 *The New Interpreter's Dictionary of the Bible, Vol. 5* (Nashville: Abingdon Press).

Schlueter, Carol J.

1994 *Filling up the Measure: Polemical Hyperbole in 1 Thessalonians 2:14-16* (JSNTSup, 98; Sheffield: JSOT Press).

Schoon-Janssen, Johannes

2000 'On the Use of Elements of Ancient Epistolography in 1 Thessalonians', in Donfried and Beutler 2000: 179-93.

Schmidt, Daryl D.

1990 'The Syntactical Style of 2 Thessalonians: How Pauline Is It?', In Collins 1990b: 383-93.

Skedros, James C.

1999 *Saint Demetrios of Thessaloniki: Civic Patron and Divine Protector 4th–7th Centuries CE* (HTS, 47; Harrisburg, PA: Trinity Press International).

Smith, Abraham

2004 'Unmasking the Powers": Toward a Postcolonial Analysis of 1 Thessalonians', in *Paul and the Roman Imperial Order* (ed. Richard A. Horsley; Harrisburg, PA: Trinity Press International).

1995 *Comfort One Another: Reconstructing the Rhetoric and Audience of 1 Thes-salonians* (Literary Currents in Biblical Interpretation; Louisville, KY: West-minster/John Knox Press).

2004 '"Unmasking the Powers": Toward a Postcolonial Analysis of 1 Thessalo-nians', in *Paul and the Roman Imperial Order* (ed. Richard A. Horsley; Har-risburg, London and New York: Trinity Press International): 47-66.

Smith, Jay E.
2001 '1 Thessalonians 4:4: Breaking the Impasse', *BBR* 11: 65-105.

Soards, Marion L.
1988 *The Apostle Paul: An Introduction to his Writings and Teaching* (New York and Mahwah: Paulist Press).

Steimle, Christopher
2008 *Religion im römischen Thessaloniki: Sakraltopographie, Kult und Gesell-schaft 168 v. Chr. – 324 n. Chr.* (STAC, 47; Tübingen: Mohr Siebeck).

Still, Todd D.
1999 *Conflict at Thessalonica: A Pauline Church and its Neighbours* (JSNTSup, 183; Sheffield: Sheffield Academic Press).

Stowers, Stanley K.
1986 *Letter Writing in Greco-Roman Antiquity* (Philadelphia: Westminster Press).

Taylor, Nicholas H.
2002 'Who Persecuted the Thessalonian Christians?', *HvTSt* 58: 784-801.

Tellbe, Mikael
2001 *Paul between Synagogue and State, Christians, Jews, and Civic Authorities in 1 Thessalonians, Romans, and Philippians* (CB, 34; Stockholm: Almqvist & Wiksell).

Trilling, Wolfgang
1972 *Untersuchungen zum zweiten Thessalonicherbrief* (Leipzig: St Benno).

Verhoef, Eduard
1997 'The Relation between 1 Thessalonians and 2 Thessalonians and the Inau-thenticity of 2 Thessalonians', *HvTSt* 53: 163-71.

Vos, Craig Steven de
1999 *Church and Community Conflicts: The Relationships of the Thessalonian, Corinthian, and Philippian Churches with their Wider Civic Communities* (SBLDS, 168; Atlanta: Scholars Press).

Walton, Steve
1995 'What Has Aristotle to Do with Paul? Rhetorical Criticism and 1 Thessalo-nians', *TynBul* 46: 229-50.

Wanamaker, Charles A.
1990 *The Epistles to the Thessalonians: A Commentary on the Greek Text* (NIGTC; Grand Rapids: Eerdmans).

2000 'Epistolary vs. Rhetorical Analysis: Is a Synthesis Possible?', in Donfried and Beutler 2000: 255-86.

2005 '"1 Thessalonians" and "2 Thessalonians"', in *Theological Interpretation of the New Testament: A Book-by-Book Survey* (ed. Kevin J. Vanhoozer, Daniel J. Treier and N.T. Wright; Grand Rapids: Baker): 148-54, 155-61.

Ware, James
1992 'The Thessalonians as a Missionary Congregation: 1 Thessalonians 1,5-8', *ZNW* 83: 126-31.

Weatherly, Jon A.
　1991　'The Authenticity of 1 Thessalonians 2:13-16: Additional Evidence', *JSNT*
　　　　42: 79-98.
Weima, Jeffery A.D., and Stanley E. Porter
　1998　*An Annotated Bibliography of 1 and 2 Thessalonians* (NTTS, 26; Leiden and
　　　　Boston: Brill).
Whitton, J.
　1982　'A Neglected Meaning for skeuos in 1 Thessalonians 4.4'. *NTS* 28: 142-43.
Winter, Bruce W.
　1989　'"If a man does not wish to work...": A Cultural and Historical Setting for
　　　　2 Thessalonians 3:6-16', *TynBul* 40: 303-15.
Witherington III, Ben
　2006　*1 and 2 Thessalonians: A Socio-Rhetorical Commentary* (Grand Rapids:
　　　　Eerdmans).
Witmer, Stephen E.
　2006　'"θεοδίδακτοι" in 1 Thessalonians 4.9: A Pauline Neologism', *NTS* 52: 239-
　　　　50.
Wrede, William
　1903　*Die Echtheit des zweiten Thessalonicherbriefs untersucht* (TUGAL, 24/2;
　　　　Leipzig: Henrichs).
Yarbro Collins, Adela
　1986　'Introduction: Early Christian Apocalypticism', *Semeia* 36: 1-11.

1 and 2 Thessalonians

Index of Subjects

antichrist 81
apocalypse 16, 52-56, 81
apocalyptic 15, 16, 52-53, 60, 70-71, 74,
    81-82
Aristotle 28, 58
artisan 8, 9, 11, 16, 40, 42
associations 4, 10-12, 15, 21, 38, 40-43,
    50-51, 53-54, 75, 76
ataktos see disruption
atheism 14, 43
Athens 4, 21, 22, 40, 50, 76, 78
Augustus 18
authorship 5, 19-21, 57-61, 65, 67

banquet *see meal*
beast 81
benefaction *see patronage*
brotherly love 18, 24, 30, 49-50
burial 11, 51, 52, 53-54

Cabirus 12
child/children 14, 36, 37, 48, 52
childbirth 52, 55
clean/unclean *see purity/pollution*
collectivism 15, 21, 44, 49
Corinth 8, 20, 21, 22, 33, 40, 49, 56, 76,
    78, 79
Corinthians, 3rd 58
Cynic 39

Dead Sea Scrolls 48
death 5, 9, 11, 14, 21, 34, 52-55, 76, 79
Diocletian 79
Dionysos 51, 53, 54
Dioscuri 12, 49
disruption 61, 65, 74-77
distress 65

Egypt 14, 76
emperor 3, 51, 69, 70, 73
emperor worship *see imperial cult*

Enoch 53
epistolography *see letter writing*

family 10, 14, 37, 42, 53
funeral *see burial*

Galerius 79
genitalia 48
Gentile 9, 16, 25-26, 73
God-fearer 16
Gospel of Thomas 58
group formation 3, 11-12

Hades 53
honorific practices 3, 11, 12, 15, 29, 33,
    36, 37, 38, 41-42, 43, 47, 50-51, 58
hospitality 14
house 3, 14, 16
household 36

idle 63, 74
idol 9, 14, 15, 41-42
imperial cult 70, 73
Isis 12, 13-14

Jesus 9, 15, 16, 18, 20, 24, 25, 26, 27, 30,
    38, 39, 42, 54-56, 57, 59, 61, 65, 67,
    68, 69, 74, 78, 81-82
Jew/Jewish 3, 9, 14, 15, 21, 25-28, 49,
    52-53, 73

Kassander 7

Laodiceans (letter to) 58
leadership 5, 21, 24, 30, 33, 37, 43-45,
    59, 80
leatherworker 8-9, 10, 51
letter writing 1, 4, 18-19, 22-24

Macedonia 6-7, 22, 39, 49
man of lawlessness 70, 81

INDEX OF AUTHORS